BACKYARD
PLAYGROUNDS

BUILD AMAZING TREEHOUSES, NINJA PROJECTS, OBSTACLE COURSES, AND MORE!

DAVID AND JEANIE STILES
DESIGNS & ILLUSTRATIONS BY DAVID STILES

Skyhorse Publishing

Skyhorse Publishing books may be purchased in bulk at special discounts for sales promotion, corporate gifts, fund-raising, or educational purposes. Special editions can also be created to specifications. For details, contact the Special Sales Department, Skyhorse Publishing, 307 West 36th Street, 11th Floor, New York, NY 10018 or info@skyhorsepublishing.com.

Skyhorse® and Skyhorse Publishing® are registered trademarks of Skyhorse Publishing, Inc.®, a Delaware corporation.

Visit our website at www.skyhorsepublishing.com.

10 9 8 7 6 5 4 3

Library of Congress Cataloging-in-Publication Data is available on file.

Cover design by Daniel Brount
Cover image by David and Jeanie Stiles

Print ISBN: 978-1-5107-6328-9
Ebook ISBN: 978-1-5107-6665-5

Printed in China

To Toby Haynes, who helped us in so many ways,
and without whom we could not have done this book.

Contents

Part Four: Timeless DIY Projects & Games 121

Introduction

Kids and families of all ages are rediscovering the great outdoors, including their own backyards. Life has changed as a result of the pandemic and it is more important than ever to be able to entertain our kids at home, teach them about nature, and give them a great time building, exercising, staying in shape, and working together. All these actions help foster independence, confidence, and growth. In *Backyard Playgrounds,* we offer user-friendly plans and do-it-yourself projects that can be made in an afternoon—circle swing, treasure chest, four square game—as well as more ambitious projects, like the warped wall and treehouse. We show how to build a complete ninja adventure course to turn your backyard into a place where kids love to play. The treehouse doubles as a home base for the adventure course that radiates from it.

"Junkyard playgrounds" were prevalent during World War II in Copenhagen, Denmark, when it was noticed that children were playing with pieces of scrap in bomb sites. Soon after the war, the same thing happened in other countries. Similar playgrounds made their debut in New York City under the direction of Mayor John Lindsay and Thomas Hoving. Adventure playgrounds were started with the idea that children learn from experimentation and discovery—not from just sitting on a swing, but by using their own minds and bodies while having fun. One researcher who had studied playgrounds in the United States concluded, "Commercial playgrounds were designed to minimize harm (injury) rather than maximize enjoyment." In our increasingly litigious society, school playgrounds have been designed out of fear to avoid risks at all costs; however, studies show that fewer injuries have occurred at adventure playgrounds than at typical playgrounds precisely because the child is aware of the risks and is more careful.

Ninja

The history of the ninja goes back to feudal Japan, with the clandestine training of young men as mercenaries to infiltrate enemy lines at night to gather information. They had to be masters of disguise and deception, skilled in the martial art of Ninjutsu; they could scale walls, move silently and undetected, escape, and survive. The ninja were not subject to the samurai codes of honor. It was said that they had superhuman powers and could transform themselves into birds and animals.

NINJA COURSE

The four famous Teenage Mutant Ninja Turtles, trained in ninjutsu by an anthropomorphic rat, are more recent. Named after four Italian Renaissance artists, they first appeared in a 1984 comic book, and went on to become a popular television series in the 1980s and 1990s. Extremely popular video games and films followed.

More recently still, the television series *American Ninja Warrior* (based on the Japanese show *Sasuke*) shows a competition between trained athletes traversing extremely difficult obstacle courses against the clock.

Many playgrounds across the United States now feature scaled-down versions of the Ninja Warrior obstacles seen on TV. Milder versions of ninja-themed activities are offered even for preschoolers. Our take on the ninja course is described in this book.

Helpful Abbreviations

AC ply = A/C grade exterior plywood
O.C. = on center
P.T. = pressure-treated
TYP = typical

Before You Get Started

Note: Every effort has been made to design all the projects in this book with clear and easy-to-follow instructions. It is, however, impossible to predict every situation and the ability of each carpenter who builds our projects, and we advise the reader to seek advice from a competent on-site expert.

Disclaimer: David and Jeanie Stiles make no express or implied warranties, including warranties of performance, merchantability, and fitness for a particular purpose, regarding the information in this book. Your use of this information is at your own risk. You assume full responsibility and risk of loss resulting from the use of this information. The authors and publisher will not be responsible for any direct, special, indirect, incidental, consequential, or punitive damages or any other damage whatsoever.

It is your responsibility to know the limitations of the people using the equipment and to supervise accordingly.

Read this important safety notice: To prevent accidents, keep safety in mind while you work. Use the safety guards installed on power equipment. When working with power equipment, keep fingers away from saw blades, wear safety goggles to prevent injuries from flying wood chips and sawdust, wear hearing protection, and consider installing a dust vacuum to reduce the amount of airborne sawdust in your woodshop. Don't wear loose clothing or jewelry when working with power equipment. Tie back long hair to prevent it from getting caught in your equipment. People who are sensitive to certain chemicals should check the chemical content of any product before using it. The authors and editors who compiled this book have tried to make the contents as accurate and correct as possible. Plans, illustrations, photographs, and text have been carefully checked. All instructions, plans, and projects should be carefully read, studied, and understood before beginning construction. Due to the variability of local conditions, construction materials, skill levels, etc., neither the author nor the publisher assumes any responsibility for any accidents, injuries, damages, or other losses incurred resulting from the material presented in this book.

Part One
Backyard Ninja Adventure Course

The designs in this section have been chosen because they are versatile, adaptable, and relatively straightforward to make; for an absolute novice woodworker, the warped wall is just a little more advanced, but well within the capabilities of the average home handyperson. They've all been tested and approved for fun and good exercise, and are easily adapted to different ages and agility levels. The climbing wall, for example, can be the focus of intense competition between your teenage ninjas, or a wonderful prop for the imaginative role-play and adventure games of much younger kids. There's always scope to make the obstacles more difficult, or easier, as required; we suggest how in the individual projects that follow.

If you're building a whole course or circuit, give yourself time to think about how the various elements fit together, and in which order; it's a good idea to follow a test of strength with a test of balance or agility, and so on. A design on paper, with rough dimensions of the available space, is a great help, but in the end nothing beats walking—or running—around the site and trying to envision the best angle of approach and length of run-up to the different obstacles. Once this is fine-tuned, you may (as we did, eventually) feel confident enough to hire a Bobcat with an auger to dig all the postholes at once, and thereby save a lot of time and effort. And if it's a circuit, don't forget to install a post or tall stake to mark the start and finish.

It's extremely important that all hardware used in the construction of play or climbing equipment be rated for such use; any old eyebolt from the store or salvaged from a corner of the shed will *not* do. The same applies to nets, ropes, and cables. There are specialist suppliers of these things, and they can also advise on suitable choices. We have dealt with:

- ropes.courses (hardware) USA
- e-rigging.com (hardware) USA
- jammarmfg.com (nets) USA

WELCOME TO THE ADVENTURE COURSE!

Please read these guidelines carefully before attempting the adventure course. Strength, agility, and focus are key to safe & successful use of this equipment; challenge yourself but be aware of your skill level; don't take on too much before you are ready. Never engage in the adventure-course activities while under the influence of alcohol or drugs, or if impaired in any way. The obstacles are only to be used by authorized persons, under adult supervision at all times, and only in dry conditions (as surfaces may become slippery when wet).

Uneven Monkey Bars
- A spotter is required for individual under 5' tall.
- Spotter should follow and assist the user as necessary.
- From mounting location, take hold of the first bar and work your way to the last bar, hand over hand. Use the dismount rope if necessary upon completion.
- Do not leap from mounting location onto distant bars.
- Do not climb on or hang from wooden components of the structure—you might get splinters.

Nitro Swing
- From start platform, gain a position with your weight on the circular rope stand or by holding on to the rope, and swing from one platform to the other.
- Platforms can be moved farther apart to increase the difficulty.
- Be careful of the rope stand as you dismount—it may bump into your shins.

Shaky Log
- Only one person at a time may use the obstacle.
- From the start platform, grab hold of the first rope and step onto the log. Work your way across to the last platform without touching the ground.
- Be careful, as the shaky logs move unpredictably and may bump into each other or the posts . . . or you!

Swing into Cargo Net

- A spotter is required. Spotter should be positioned to catch the swing once the user launches into the net. This will protect the user from potential collision with the returning swing.
- Stand on the swing and build up enough momentum to catch the cargo net and let go of the swing. After grasping the cargo net, work your way hand over hand and foot over foot down the net and along the underside to the dropping point without touching the ground. If you can't make it to the dropping point, just lower your feet into the wood-chip bed and stand up.
- Do not climb up the net and sit on the crossbars—this height exceeds allowable height for users without a safety harness.
  Note: There are 4-swing-attachment positions for the swing, to make the obstacle easier or harder.

Rope Wall Climb

- A spotter is required for users under 5' tall. Spotter should assist the user on both sides of the wall.
- The obstacle can be surmounted by climbing hand over hand or by using the knots as rungs. Dismount the same way.

Warped Wall

- Make sure the wall is free of dust & debris before each use.
- A spotter is required for users under 5' tall.
- Wear sneakers with good rubber soles that are clean & dry.
- Run at the wall at full speed; upon contact, transfer your energy upward to project yourself up. Grab hold of the top rail and hoist yourself over the top.
- Exit the obstacle by using the ladder at the back of the wall, making sure to have at least 3 points of contact (hand & feet) as you climb down.

WARPED WALL

No ninja course is complete without a warped wall. The runners use their forward momentum to gain height in order to reach the top. We recommend going to an adventure park before planning your wall to find out what your athletic level is and how high a wall you can handle. We recently built one for a family with younger and older teens; it has a 12' and a 9' warped wall side by side. The following plans are for a 10' version, but we also describe this double wall. The principle is the same for any height. We recommend using 1" marine plywood for outdoor use. The example in our photographs is made of marine meranti, which is expensive but durable and looks great. Take care to rout and sand all exposed edges of the plywood and ladder—this really is a hands-on structure.

MATERIALS

4	4×4×12' P.T.	Supports
2	2×4×12' P.T.	Ladder
3	2×4×8' P.T.	Rungs
3	2×4×8' P.T.	Framing ledges
9	2×4×8' P.T.	Cross braces
5	4'×8' 1" marine ply	Sides, top, and back
5	4'×8' ¼" marine ply	Front
1	4' 1½" dia. PVC pipe	Grab rail
1	Gallon epoxy resin with slow hardener	
1	1×2×10' pine	Compass beam
4	Bags concrete mix	Postholes
	2½" and 3½" deck screws	

Instructions

Frame

Dig four holes and concrete the 12' 4×4 posts 2' deep in the ground to form a rectangle 30"×46" (outside dimensions). Make sure the posts are exactly aligned and vertical so the structure will measure 48" across when the two 1" plywood sides are added. You may find it easier to concrete only one (rear) post in place at this stage. You can leave the others standing loose in the holes until the sides and back are attached, to allow for any necessary adjustments. **(See Fig. 1.)**

Cutting the Curve

(See Fig. 2.) Lay two sheets of 1" plywood on a level surface as shown in illustration. Clamp them together with 2×4s underneath, making sure these supports won't interfere with the blade of your jigsaw later. Measure 8' from the two corners marked A and B in illustration and hammer a short stake into the ground at this point.

Make a compass beam from a 10' 1×2. Near one end, drill a hole just big enough to hold a pencil. Drive a 3" nail through the other end, 8' from the hole, and hammer the nail into the stake. Draw the curve onto the plywood; use a jigsaw to cut out the curve. Do the same for the second sidewall. Check that the two sides match, and sand as necessary until the curve is smooth.

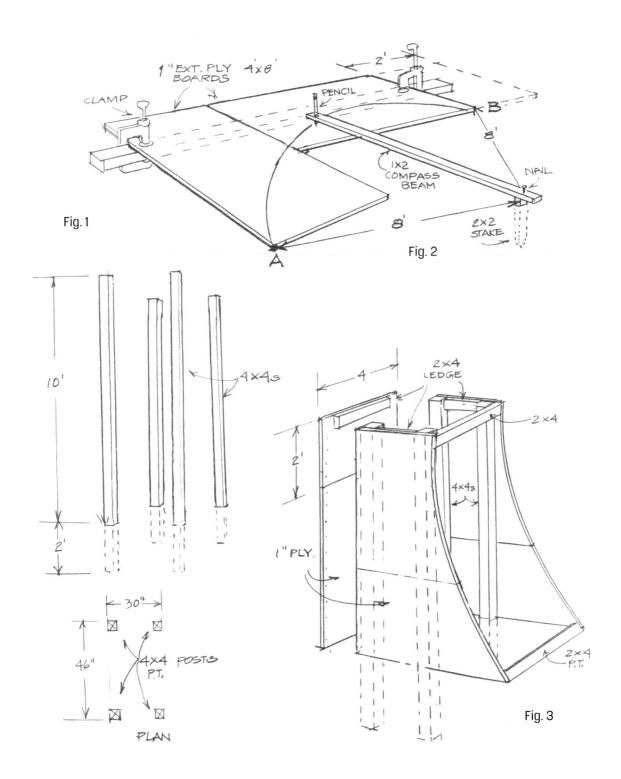

Fig. 1

1" EXT. PLY 4'x8'
BOARDS

CLAMP

PENCIL

2'

B

8'

1X2
COMPASS
BEAM

NAIL

8'

2X2
STAKE

A

Fig. 2

10'

4X4s

2'

30"

46"

4X4 POSTS
P.T.

PLAN

2X4
LEDGE

4'

2'

2X4

4X4s

1" PLY.

2X4
P.T.

Fig. 3

Attaching the Sides and Back

Clamp the first lower panel to the posts, check the levels, and attach with 2½" deck screws. Do the same for the other side. Clamp and adjust the panel as necessary to make sure the frame remains square and the two sides are the same height. This is especially important, as the curved front of the wall will not fit properly otherwise. Align and secure the upper panels on both sides. **(See Fig. 3.)**

Attach a sheet of 1" plywood across the back of the structure, lining it up with the bottom edges of the sides. It should fit flush with both sides. Cut a 2'×4' piece of plywood to complete the back. Screw the two 2×4 ladder sides securely to the plywood with 3½" deck screws, working from inside. The two rails extend above the wall to provide grab rails when descending the ladder. Space them to suit the size and age of the users— probably around 15–18" apart. Attach rungs of 2×4 using 3½" deck screws (two per end). Set the top rung below the top of the wall (as shown on **Fig. 4**), where it won't impede descent. When we built our first wall, the side rails ended flush with the platform, but we immediately realized that grab rails were needed, as the ladder is used almost exclusively for climbing down (backward) rather than up. The rails extend 30" above the platform and 18" below, securely fastened at several points to the outside of the ladder rails; this method also leaves the gap between grab rails wider than the ladder, for ease of access.

Cut a piece of 1" plywood for the platform and attach it to the top.

If you haven't already done so, concrete the remaining posts in place now.

Building the Front Wall

(See Fig. 4 and Fig. 5.) Cut the 2×4 cross braces to 46" and attach on edge between the curved sides of the wall at 8" intervals, using 3½" screws. The lowest one is face-on (as shown) to fit the narrow space at the bottom of the wall. We used an additional cross brace to bridge the junction between upper and lower side panels (to keep everything aligned), and another where the upper and lower panels of the curved wall would meet.

Since you will be attaching three layers of ¼" plywood to the frame, you need to make sure the screws don't run into each other. We did this by marking lines lengthways on the plywood, offsetting the center screws by 2" to the right on the first layer, 2" to the left on the second, and centered on the third (outer) layer. At the sides we marked successive layers 6", 4", and 2" from the edge.

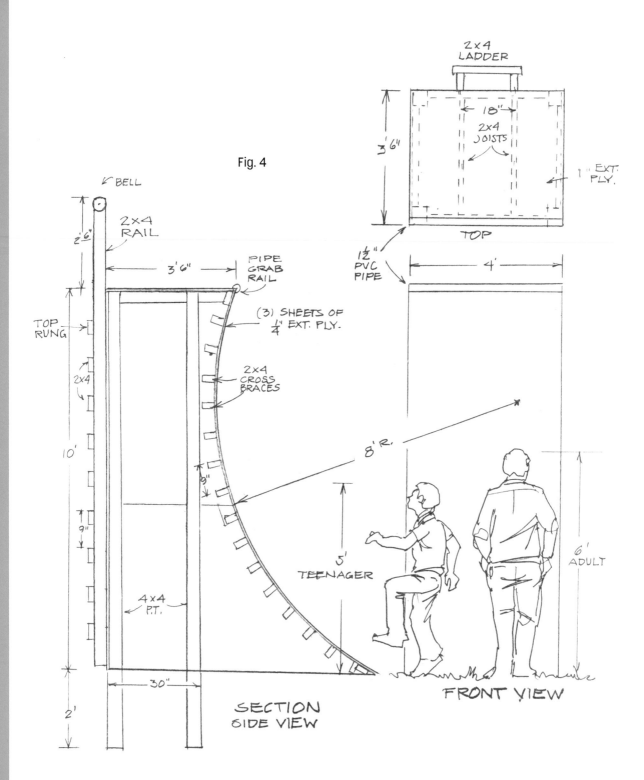

Fig. 4

BELL

2×4
RAIL

2'6"

PIPE
GRAB
RAIL

3'6"

(3) SHEETS OF
¼" EXT. PLY.

TOP
RUNG

2×4
CROSS
BRACES

2×4

8'R.

10'

8"

9"

5'
TEENAGER

4×4
P.T.

30"

2'

SECTION
SIDE VIEW

2×4
LADDER

18"
2×4
JOISTS

3'6"

1" EXT.
PLY.

TOP

1½"
PVC
PIPE

4'

6'
ADULT

FRONT VIEW

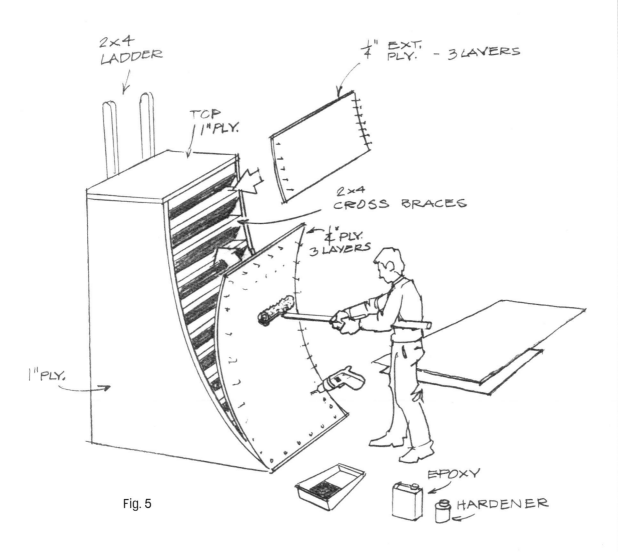

2×4
LADDER

TOP
1" PLY.

¼" EXT.
PLY. – 3 LAYERS

2×4 CROSS BRACES

¼" PLY.
3 LAYERS

1" PLY.

EPOXY

HARDENER

Fig. 5

Attaching the front of the wall is much easier with two or three people. Apply exterior adhesive to the cross braces and the curved edges of the sides, and screw the first panel of ¼" plywood to the bottom cross brace, using 2½" deck screws. Bend the panel into the curve, using your heaviest friend, and attach to all the cross braces in sequence from bottom to top, making sure the edges are flush with the side panels all the way up. You can locate the crossbraces beneath the ¼" plywood by marking a horizontal line across it, from each pair of screw holes in the side panels. Cut a second panel to fit the top of the curve and fasten the same way.

To stagger the joins, cut the lower panel of the second layer the same size as the upper panel of the first. The radius of the curve decreases fractionally with each layer, so the upper panels will end up slightly long, but in practice it's best to let this happen and cut/sand flush afterward. They will be bonded to the first layer with marine epoxy (we used the West System, with slow hardener). If you've not used this before, take time to read and fully understand the instructions and precautions before you begin, and make sure you have everything ready at the outset.

Using a roller, coat the section of the first layer that will be covered by the lower panel of the second; attach as before. Align and attach the second upper panel.

Repeat for the third layer, staggering the join again. Take special care aligning the panels, as this is the surface the runners will be using.

Finishing

Rout and sand all edges thoroughly and apply three coats of epoxy to the curved face of the wall.

The top edge of the wall is covered with PVC pipe to give the runners' hands protection and extra grip. **(See Fig. 6.)** Cut out a section of the pipe about ⅓ of the circumference, fill with a mixture of epoxy and sawdust, and screw to the top of the wall using countersunk screws; be careful to leave no sharp edges here.

Excavate the area around the sides and back of the wall to a depth of 12", and fill with bark chips.

Double Warped Wall

We were just finishing the 12' wall shown in the photos when the clients had second thoughts about its height—they worried that it might be too ambitious for their kids. This is why we strongly advise you to assess your capabilities before you start building. We discussed "simply" cutting it down two feet (a possible if untidy solution), but decided instead to attach a second, lower wall to it. In the event, the older kids quickly graduated to the big wall, but the adaptation makes it more versatile. It's constructed in the same way, except that the cross braces are "toe-screwed" into the side of the big wall. The main consideration was to match the curved face perfectly to the existing one. To do this we clamped the new side panels to the first structure (bringing them forward ¾" to allow for the thickness of the plywood front) and traced the curve. We also took special care to position the new panels exactly in line with the others. We routed the inner edge of the third layer of ¼" plywood before attaching it, as it would not be accessible afterward.

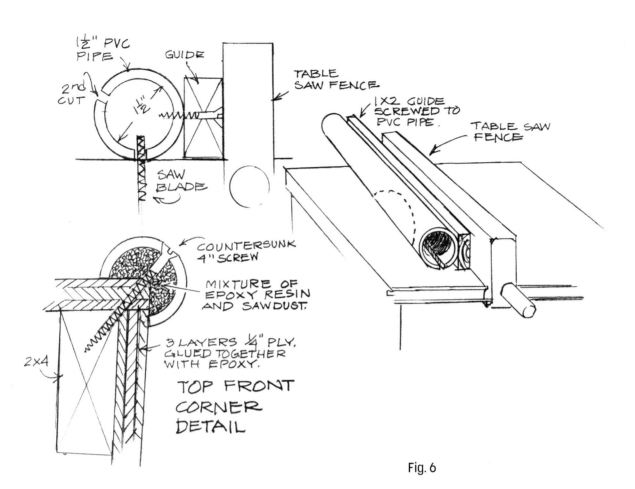

1½" PVC PIPE

GUIDE

2nd CUT

1½"

TABLE SAW FENCE

SAW BLADE

1X2 GUIDE SCREWED TO PVC PIPE.

TABLE SAW FENCE

COUNTERSUNK 4" SCREW

MIXTURE OF EPOXY RESIN AND SAWDUST.

3 LAYERS ¼" PLY, GLUED TOGETHER WITH EPOXY.

2X4

TOP FRONT CORNER DETAIL

Fig. 6

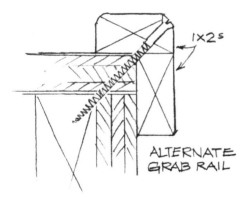

1X2s

ALTERNATE GRAB RAIL

NITRO SWING

The humble rope swing gets a lot more exciting when it involves a leap across a deadly chasm from one small safe perch to another! The platforms turn recreation into adventure activity. Concerned parents might choose (as we did) to replace the crocodiles and postapocalyptic chemicals with a deep layer of bark chips and a healthy dose of imagination, but the challenge remains. There's plenty of scope to vary the difficulty by moving the platforms farther apart or making them a different size, for example; ours are about 24"×30" and 8" high. If you plan to go much smaller, make the sides out of 2×6s or 2×4s, or they may become too "tippy." The Nitro Swing is great for team games: the whole team has to transfer from one side to the other (one at a time, folks), with perhaps a time penalty for anyone who touches down in the toxic gloop. In this scenario you could either have a length of thin cord attached to the bottom of the swing for the next team member to retrieve the rope or make it the responsibility of the landing party to swing it back. For the youngest kids, do away with platforms altogether, and just let them burn some of that surplus energy on the swing. **(See Fig. 1.)**

The longer the rope, the better the swing. We used 16' posts for this one. They must also be set far enough apart to prevent collisions.

LUMBER

Qty.	Size	Description	Length	Location
2	6×6	P.T. lumber	16'	Support posts
1	6×6	P.T. lumber	10'	Crossbeam
1	4×4	P.T. lumber	8'	Braces
1	2×8	P.T. lumber	10'	Platform frame
1	2×8	P.T. lumber	8'	Platform frame
2	$5/4$×6	P.T. lumber	10'	Platform top
1	1"	Marine plywood	9" circle	Swing foothold
1	$3/4$"	Rope with thimble	14'	Swing
1	$5/8$"	Eyebolt	7"	Swing attachment
1	$3/8$"	Rapid link (maillon)		Swing attachment
2	$5/8$"	Lag screws	12"	Crossbeam attachment
2	8"	Angle brackets, screws		Crossbeam attachment
4	$5/8$"	Lag screws	6"	Brace attachment

Instructions

Prepare the 6×6 and 4×4 lumber by routing the edges and sanding.

Dig the first posthole. We set our 16' post about 3' deep, using quick-set concrete. The second post is (inside to inside) 8'6" from the first. Make sure they're upright, with the faces aligned. **(See Fig. 2.)**

When the concrete has set, check the levels and trim the taller post to match the shorter.

The 10' crossbeam will overhang each post by a few inches—it just looks better that way. Fit an 8" angle bracket inside the frame at each corner, and a 12" lag screw (with washer and lock-washer) vertically through the beam into the support post.

Cut two 4×4 corner braces to 4' long with 45-degree angles at the ends; attach them to the posts and crossbeam with countersunk ⅝"×6" lag screws.

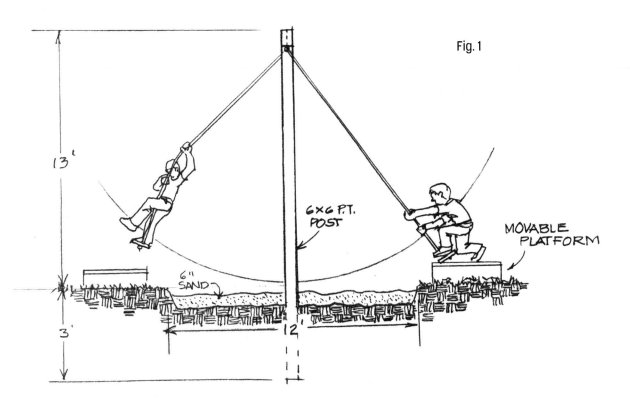

Fig. 1

6×6 P.T. POST

6" SAND

MOVABLE PLATFORM

13'

3'

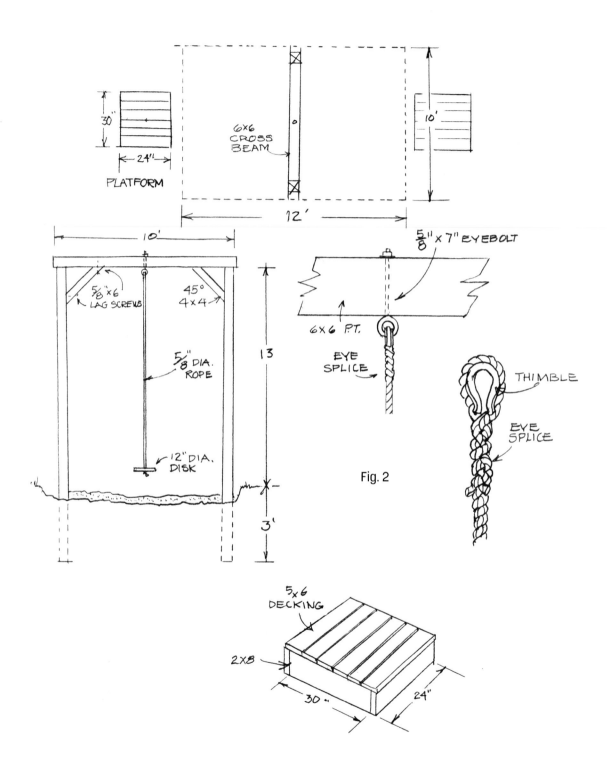

30"

← 24" →

PLATFORM

6X6
CROSS
BEAM

10'

12'

10'

5/8"×6
LAG SCREWS

45°
4×4

5/8" DIA.
ROPE

13

12" DIA.
DISK

3'

5/8" × 7" EYEBOLT

6×6 P.T.

EYE
SPLICE

Fig. 2

THIMBLE

EYE
SPLICE

5×6
DECKING

2×8

30"

24"

In the middle of the crossbeam, drill a vertical hole for the eyebolt; fit the bolt with a washer and nut. Attach the rapid link and rope with thimble. We bought our rope ready-spliced around the thimble from www.rope.courses.

Using a jigsaw, cut a 9" circle of 1" marine plywood. Drill a hole in the middle for the rope; rout and sand the edges carefully. Thread the plywood onto the rope, tie a knot underneath, and adjust till the foothold clears the ground with someone standing on it. (Option: tie a length of thin cord to the rope beneath the plywood so the next team member can haul the swing back. We deliberately kept the weight down for safety, but this pendulum will quickly lose momentum.)

Cut two lengths of 2×8 to 30", and two more to 21". Join them into a frame 24"×30" with 3½" deck screws. Cut four pieces of ⁵⁄₄×6 decking to 30", and attach to the top of the frame with 2½" screws. Remove all sharp edges with a router, and sand with the usual diligence.

Dig out the landing area to a depth of 12" and refill with bark chips.

SHAKY LOGS

Here's a nice demonstration of the difference between "simple" and "easy": to get from one platform to the other, you have to work your way along the three suspended boards without stepping off—just when you thought you'd escaped the crocodiles and noxious pools of primordial sludge. The steps are only inches from the ground but they bounce, sway, swing, and twist almost as if they *wanted* to make it difficult. . . . You can make this more or less of a challenge by adjusting the tension of the cable and by repositioning the tops of the ropes. In our photo, you can see that the middle ropes are closer together at the top, which makes this step tend to rotate more than the others; it's a bit like trying to climb from one boat to another. We built the end platforms out of 2×6s to be lower and extra stable. This is another ideal base for against-the-clock team competition; how many kids can fit on the platform?

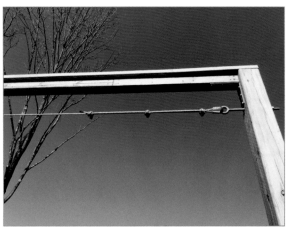

LUMBER

Qty.	Size	Description	Length	Location
2	6×6	P.T. lumber	14'	Support posts
1	2×6	P.T. lumber	18'	Top rail
2	2×4	P.T. lumber	16'	Top rail support
1	2×4	P.T. lumber	8'	Top rail support
2	2×6	P.T. lumber	10'	Platform frames
2	5/4×6	P.T. lumber	10'	Platform tops
3	1"	Marine plywood	12"×48"	Shaky log steps
6	3/4"	Rope	20'	Shaky logs
1	3/8"	Cable	25'	Shaky log suspension system
2	3/8"	Thimbles		Cable ends
12	3/8"	Cable clamps		Cable
6	5/8"	Rapid link (maillon)		Cable to rope
2	8"	Angle brackets		Top rail to posts
2	5/8"	Lag screws	8"	Top rail to posts
2	5/8"	Eyebolts	12"	Cable to posts
4	2×2	Square washers		Screws & bolts

Instructions

Prepare the lumber by routing the edges and thoroughly sanding all surfaces. We never get tired of saying this. **(See Fig. 1.)**

Dig the first posthole about 3' deep and set the post using quick-set concrete. Repeat for the second post so that the two are 20' outside to outside, vertical and carefully aligned.

Almost all the pressure on the posts is inward, from the tension and load on the cable; instead of guy wires anchored to the ground at the ends, we installed a top rail to hold the posts in position—a neat and tidy solution. Suitable lumber was not available in 20' lengths but it was easy to sister them.

Trim two 2×4s to 16' and stack them together, offset as shown so that their combined total length is 19'1". Join them using two 2½" deck screws every 12". Cut two sections of 2×4 to 3'1" and use them to "sister" the ends of the rail.

Cut a 2×6 to 18', and another to 2'. With the sistered 2×4s on edge, place the 2×6s flat on top, butted together and overhanging the sisters by 5½" at each end. Secure the 2×6s with two 3½" deck screws every 12".

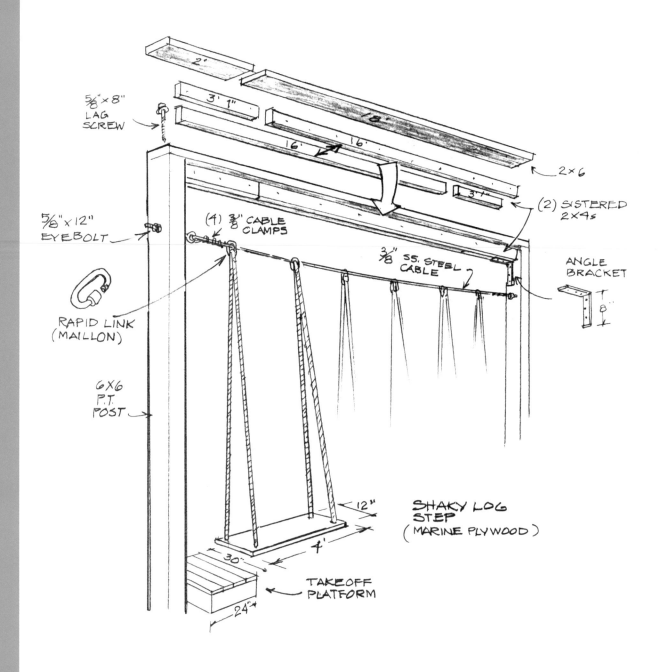

2'

5/8" × 8"
LAG
SCREW

3' 1"

18'

16"   16"

3' 4"

2×6

(2) SISTERED
2×4s

5/8" × 12"
EYEBOLT

(4) 3/8" CABLE
CLAMPS

3/8" SS. STEEL
CABLE

ANGLE
BRACKET

8"

RAPID LINK
(MAILLON)

6X6
P.T.
POST

12"

SHAKY LOG
STEP
(MARINE PLYWOOD)

30"

4'

TAKEOFF
PLATFORM

24"

Fig. 1

Lift the rail assembly onto the posts. The 2×6s should rest on the posts, and the 2×4s fit neatly between. Toe-screw the 2×4s to the post, in case they decide to wander off. Drill and fit a ⅝"×8" lag screw and washer down through the top of the 2×6 into the post, and an 8" angle bracket under either of the sistered rails.

Just below the bracket, drill a horizontal ⅝" hole from the inside face of the post to the outside. Insert a 12" eyebolt from the inside, and attach a washer and nut to the end. Make sure all the hardware for this project is properly rated for play or climbing equipment—***do not use anything else***. Check out ropes.courses and e-rigging.com for hardware.

Thread a ⅜" thimble through the eyebolt and run one end of the cable through. Temporarily hold it in place with a hand-tightened cable clamp. The simple mnemonic for cable clamps is: never saddle a dead horse—that is, the saddle (the flat part of the clamp) must be on the "live" (long) end of the cable, while the "U" grips the "dead" (tail) end. Thread the other end of the cable, and adjust so that the cable is centered. Gradually pull the cable as tight as you can by hand, then (saddling only the live horses) attach three equidistant clamps at either end. The cable can now be tensioned as required by tightening the eyebolts, but leave the final adjustment until you've made and attached the shaky log steps.

Cut three pieces of 1" marine plywood, 12"×48"; round the corners with a jigsaw, rout and sand the edges so they won't bite anyone's ankles. Drill a ¾" hole 2" in from each corner. Thread a rope through each end, tied underneath in a loose knot. (You will need to adjust for length once it's in place.)

Hook a "maillon" rapid link (carabiner) through each rope and attach to the cable; you can finger-tighten the threaded gate at this stage but it must be fully closed with a wrench at the end of installation. When all the steps are hung, experiment with cable tension, length of rope, and location of the maillons; remember that heavier ninjas will make the cable sag more, so test the setup with your big people. Use extra cable clamps as stops to keep the top of the ropes where you want them.

The take-off and landing perches we made are 24"×30". If you're planning team games, adjust the size accordingly, or: cut two pieces of 2×6 to 30" and two to 21", join with 3½" deck screws through the corners. Make the top from four pieces of ⁵⁄₄×6 cut to 30", attached with 2½" screws. Lose all the sharp edges by routing and sanding.

This adventure takes place at around the same elevation as a pair of platform shoes, but dig out the ground underneath to a depth of 12" and replace it with bark chips.

SWING INTO CARGO NET

It's harder to climb a net than a ladder, because rope absorbs more energy than solid rungs—but hey, that's a good thing, so build this and let them swarm the rigging. It's a test of agility that involves hanging from the underside of the net too: the user or competitor has to stand on the swing, gain momentum, and jump into the vertical section of net, then climb *down* and underneath—without touching the ground—to the posts at the far end. For timing purposes, you might like to add a small bell to the final crossbeam, to be rung before dismounting. Our heavy-duty cargo net (from https://jammarmfg.com) has 12" mesh. For younger kids, a smaller mesh may be more appropriate. We used rope rather than hardware to lash the net to the frame, to keep the climbing area free of metal and because it just goes with the distinctly nautical vibe. The placement of the swing will determine how easy or otherwise it is to reach the net—you can make it so close that it's just a step from one to the other. We've built some versatility into our design by adding two beams that offer multiple attachment points for the swing, to adapt as kids grow or simply to accommodate different users. Whenever you move the swing, make sure that the rapid links at the top are fully tightened. You'll need to ensure a soft landing under the net, so dig out the ground to a depth of 12" and replace with bark chips. That will be a lot easier if you do it before installing the net.

Fig. 1

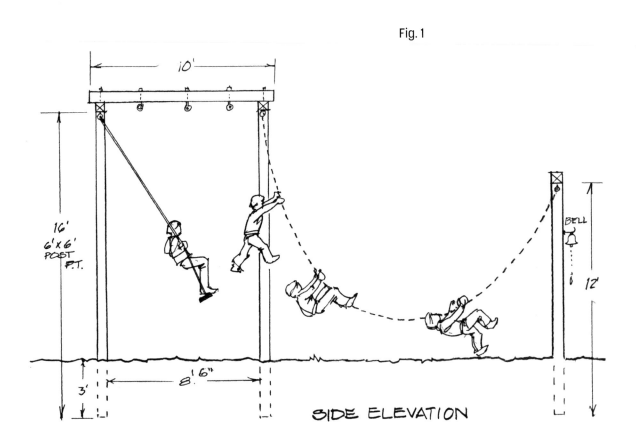

SIDE ELEVATION

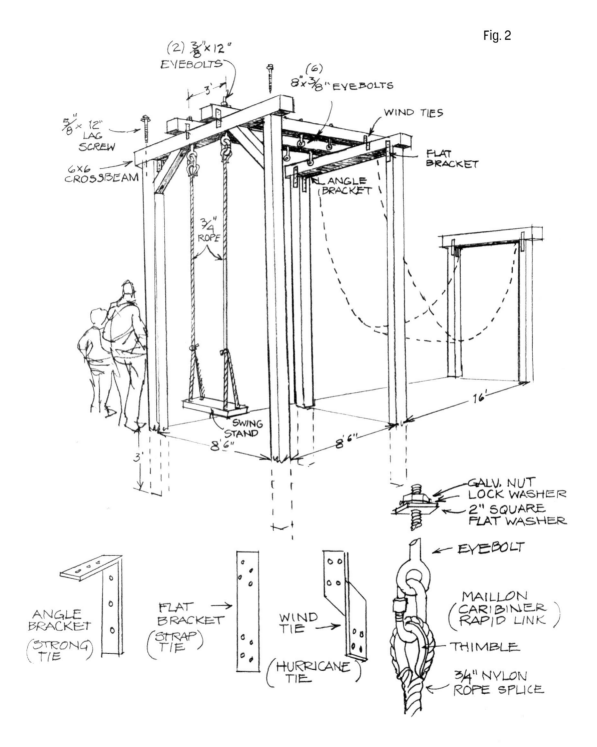

Fig. 2

(2) 3/8" x 12" EYEBOLTS

3'

(6) 8" x 3/8" EYEBOLTS

WIND TIES

5/8" x 12" LAG SCREW

FLAT BRACKET

6X6 CROSSBEAM

ANGLE BRACKET

3/4" ROPE

16'

SWING STAND

8'6"

8'6"

3'

GALV. NUT
LOCK WASHER
2" SQUARE FLAT WASHER

EYEBOLT

ANGLE BRACKET (STRONG TIE)

FLAT BRACKET (STRAP TIE)

WIND TIE (HURRICANE TIE)

MAILLON (CARIBINER RAPID LINK)

THIMBLE

3/4" NYLON ROPE SPLICE

LUMBER

Qty.	Size	Description	Length	Location
4	6×6	P.T. lumber	16'	Support posts
2	6×6	P.T. lumber	12'	Support posts
5	6×6	P.T. lumber	10'	Beams, crossbeams
1	4×4	P.T. lumber	8'	Braces
1	1"	Marine plywood	10"×24"	Swing
1	1"	Cargo net	8'×24'	Net
1	¾"	Rope	50'	Net to beams
2	¾"	Rope and thimble	18'	Swing
6		Angle brackets	8"	Beam to post
8		Flat brackets	12"	Beam to post
2	⅝"	Lag screws	12"	Beam to post
2	½"	Lag screws	6"	Brace to beam
2	⅜"	Eyebolts	12"	Beam to swing
6	⅜"	Eyebolts	8"	Beam to swing
4		Wind-ties		Beam to crossbeam
Make sure to buy washers for all lag screws and bolts.				

Instructions

Prepare the lumber by rounding the edges and sanding smooth. Really smooth. **(See Fig. 1 and Fig. 2.)**

Dig holes 3' deep for the four 16' 6×6s, so that they'll form a square 8'6" inside to inside. Set the posts with quick-set concrete, making sure they're aligned and vertical. Once the concrete is set, trim the posts to the same height.

Dig two more holes 16' from the square and in line with it. Set the two 12' posts, and trim the taller one to match the shorter.

Place a 10' crossbeam on each pair of posts and secure with 8" galvanized angle brackets.

On the four posts that will support the ends of the net, add 12" flat brackets on front and back faces to reinforce the connection.

Cut two 4' diagonal braces and attach to the posts and crossbeam that will hold the swing. Drill and attach ⅝"×12" lag screws through the crossbeam into the posts.

Lift the two remaining 10' 6×6s onto the crossbeams between swing and net. Set them parallel, at right angles to the beams, about 3' apart but not directly above the top of the braces—you will be drilling through both beams to fit the eyebolts from which the swing hangs. Once the beams are in place, fasten them with a wind-tie at each end. Drill vertically through both beams and fit the two 12" eyebolts, using a 2" square washer at each end, followed by a lock washer and nut on the threaded end.

Attach three pairs of 8" eyebolts to the two parallel beams; you can either just space them regularly or make a dummy swing with a loop of rope at the top that you can slide along the beam to test it. Establish the default position of the swing and attach two spliced ropes (fitted with thimbles) to the corresponding eyebolts, using a rapid link fully locked.

Cut the plywood for the swing stand. Round off the corners with a jigsaw, rout and sand the edges, and drill four holes for the rope. At each end, thread the rope through one hole and back through the other. Tie off the rope two or three feet above the stand.

Dig out the ground and replace with 12" of bark chips.

Temporarily clamp or tie one end of the net to the middle crossbeam. Securely lash a ¾" rope to the end of the beam and thread it through every loop of the net to the opposite side. Don't worry about tightening it all in one go. Rope can be tiring stuff to work with, and it will fight you all the way—work your way to the end, then go back and take up the slack loop by loop. Tie off the far end and trim any excess rope. Repeat at the far end of the net.

Jumping into the net is easier if the top section is more or less vertical. We used two sets of simple loops to make this adjustment.

ROPE

CLIMBING WALL

This climbing wall is built for adventure—simple, sturdy, with no sharp hardware. Be especially diligent with your sanding on this one, and check all boards for cracks and rough bits before incorporating them. Our wall stands about 8'3" high (depending where you measure from—it's on a slight slope) but the design can easily be scaled up or down. **(See Fig. 1.)** In this case, we suggest adjusting length and width as well as height in proportion. If climbing the wall is not sufficient challenge for team games, you could perhaps get the teams to transport buckets of water over the wall and fill a container to a specified level, against the clock; we do *not* recommend imitating the famous Royal Navy Field Gun Race, even if you have a spare 12-pounder cannon. Check this out on YouTube!

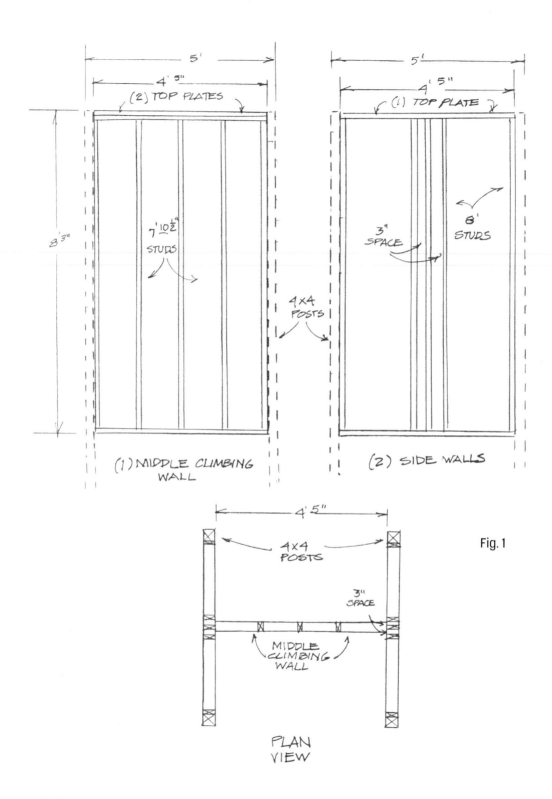

5'

4' 5"

(2) TOP PLATES

8' 3"

7' 10½"
STUDS

4×4
POSTS

(1) MIDDLE CLIMBING
WALL

5'

4' 5"

(1) TOP PLATE

3"
SPACE

8'
STUDS

(2) SIDE WALLS

4' 5"

4×4
POSTS

3"
SPACE

MIDDLE
CLIMBING
WALL

PLAN
VIEW

Fig. 1

LUMBER

Qty.	Size	Description	Length	Location
4	4×4	P.T. lumber	12'	Support posts
15	2×4	P.T. lumber	8'	Frame
4	2×4	P.T. lumber	10'	Frame
60	⁵⁄₄×6	P.T. lumber	10'	Walls, trim
2	1"	Rope	12'	Climbing wall

Instructions

Dig holes for the four support posts, to form a rectangle 5'×5' outside to outside. No one will refuse to play if the structure isn't perfectly square, but accuracy is a good habit and makes things fit together more easily. The holes should be at least 30" deep. Set the posts using quick-set concrete, checking the levels and angles as you go.

Cut the top and bottom plates from 10' 2×4s for the first side, to fit inside the two posts, at 4'5". Cut five more 8' 2×4s to 8' for the verticals (studs). Attach the two end studs flush with

the ends of the top and bottom plates. Use two 3½" deck screws per junction, and make sure the frame is square. Add a stud at the midpoint of the plates, and another 3" away from this on either side; these extra studs will be nailers for the inside wall boards. Lift the frame into place, check that the top is horizontal, and screw the outer studs to the posts. Repeat for the opposite side, making sure the two sides are the same height. Trim the tops of the posts flush with the frames.

For the connecting wall (the actual climbing part) the top and bottom plates will be 4'5". Cut three, as the top will be doubled to reinforce the rope attachment. The five studs are 7'10½" to allow for this. Make the frame, and attach the second top plate using 2½" screws afterward. When fitting this plate, keep the screws clear of the middle 9", as you'll be drilling through the double plate to thread the rope later, and drills don't like screws. Align the frame with the two sides and screw it to the middle studs.

Cut ⁵⁄₄×6s to 5' long, to fit across the climbing wall and finish flush with the end of the side studs. The bottom board needs to be notched out to fit over the bottom plates at each end; the notch is 3½" along the grain and 1" across. Attach the boards to the studs with two 2½" screws per stud. Build several courses the same way on both faces of the wall, then begin to make the outside walls to firm up the structure. Add the inside faces of the sidewalls last, as they overlap the climbing wall. When you reach the top, stop! If necessary, rip the top course to end flush with the top plate; if the adjustment is minor, you may be able to finagle it with some judicious spacing of the boards, but please, no 2" gaps. The last board of the climbing wall will require another little notch at the ends, to fit under the top plate.

Cut and attach ⁵⁄₄×6 facing boards on the ends of the walls. Do the same for the top of the sidewalls. Cut another piece to complete the climbing wall.

Before attaching it, carefully rout and sand the ends for the comfort of your athletes.

Drill two holes through the climbing wall, 3" from the top and 3" to either side of the midpoint. Thread a 1" rope from each side, knotted securely at the top. Tie several knots equidistantly down the ropes.

Dig out the ground below the wall on both sides to a depth of 12", and replace with bark chips.

MONKEY BARS

Monkey bars are understandably popular with monkeys everywhere. We've added a detail or two to make it more interesting for the whole troop. The 2×12 top beams allow the bars to be set asymmetrically on both vertical and horizontal planes. Try to experiment with different configurations before fixing permanently—for example, you might want to make the right-hand side of the course much more of a stretch than the left; for younger kids, perhaps use slightly thinner pipe. Your smaller monkeys will appreciate the ladder and rope to help them reach the first bar. If that's too easy, consider replacing the ladder with a knotted rope hung from an extra bar at the starting end. We built ours 12' long, but you can make it as long as you want by adding sections, whether in a straight line, snaking, or forming a continuous loop. In the latter case, of course, the bars will have to be more widely spaced on the outer side of the circuit, like the spokes of a wheel.

LUMBER

Qty.	Size	Description	Length	Location
4	6×6	P.T. lumber	12'	Support posts
4	2×12	P.T. lumber	12'	Top beams
1	2×6	P.T. lumber	8'	Ladder sides
5	1¼"	Galvanized pipe	5'	Monkey bars
3	1¼"	Galvanized pipe	4'	Ladder rungs
1	1"	Rope	20'	Hand holds
12	½"	Lag screws	6"	Rails to posts

Instructions

Prepare the lumber by routing and sanding smooth—folks are going to climb on this. The 2×12 top beams should have the corners rounded with a jigsaw first. A small cup, jar, or lid often makes a good template to draw the curve before cutting, which helps to give the whole shebang a cleaner look.

Dig four postholes 3' deep, to form a rectangle 5'×11' outside to outside. Set the posts in position with quick-set concrete, making sure they're upright and aligned. Use a level to identify the lowest post, and mark the others to the same height. Cut the posts now, or wait till the beams are installed.

Clamp a 12' 2×12 top beam to the inside face of the first pair of posts, with equal overhang at both ends. Check the level, and secure to each post with two ½"×6" lag screws. Repeat with the inside beam on the other pair of posts.

Rest the 5' lengths of galvanized pipe across the top of the beam, adjust the spacings to suit, and mark the positions on the inside of the beams. Remember to mix up the heights and degree of tilt too, for added interest.

Drill holes in the beams to accept the pipe—it's worth doing a test hole in a scrap of wood to check the size; try to drill the holes in line with the chosen angle of the pipe—a stick that fits between the beams may help you to eyeball the trajectory. Thread the pipes into the beams and see how it looks. If you have to drill another hole or two to make changes, this would be the time. If you're happy with it, clamp the two outer beams in place and attach with two 3½" deck screws per post. There's no load on the outer beams (They're just to keep the pipes in place and for finish), but in case the monkeys decide to go freestyle, add a 6" lag screw per post for good measure.

For the ladder sides, cut two 2×6s to 3' long, and drill three holes in each for the galvanized rungs. Cut the rungs to length with a hacksaw and thread them onto both sides. Lift the ladder into place between the start posts and secure with two 3½" screws each at top, bottom, and middle.

Cut a length of 1" rope, tie one end over the inner beam beside the ladder, and knot the lower end. Tie another length of rope to the far end of the beam, knotted in three or four places to help small monkeys climb down at the end of the course.

Dig out the ground under the bars to a depth of 12" and replace with bark chips.

Part Two
Treehouse Headquarters (All Using One Tree)

Everyone loves a treehouse—it's a wonderful place to relax, connect with nature, and enjoy the view. But we've found that a treehouse is also a great addition to a ninja course. For one thing, there's a sense of adventure to be had from climbing even the most sedate stairs to a platform in a tree, and the different perspective it gives to a familiar scene. How much more so when there's a whole obstacle course down there! It's the perfect vantage point to follow the progress of kids—or adults—around the circuit, and is a ready-made start/finish post for such games as a race against the clock. You could hang a small bell under the platform, and the competitor has to ring it when finishing the course—timed by the race controller in the treehouse. How about an award ceremony for the winner, who is invited up onto the platform to receive the trophy? (Maybe forget the champagne-spraying thing.) This kind of event makes for truly memorable kids' parties; it's up to you to ensure your phone is juiced up in advance. This chapter gives an idea of just how simple or elaborate such a treehouse might be. The designs here are variations on a basic theme that uses a single tree, supported by either diagonal braces or two posts. At its simplest, you could easily build a platform in a weekend. If there's no suitable tree available, no problem: you can use a post in each corner instead. Budget, space, and time are always factors, but think about how you might want to use the treehouse. The simple platform is always a big hit with kids and parents, but obviously the larger spaces with covered or enclosed cabins offer even more possibilities. Some of our treehouses are fitted out with chairs, tables, and even sleeping lofts. They're especially great for families to enjoy together and with friends. It's not unheard of for people to host small dinner parties in their treehouse.

ONE, TWO, TREE-HOUSE

This simple treehouse can be built quickly and inexpensively by the average homeowner, using a minimum of tools. It is high enough for kids to feel they are up in a tree, yet low enough for parents to hand up snacks. It suits a tree over 8" in diameter.

Tools

- Tape measure
- Electric screwdriver and spade drill set (½" and ⅜")
- Handsaw or electric circular saw (Skilsaw)
- Jigsaw (optional)
- Hammer
- Socket wrench (¾")
- Carpenter's level
- Framing square

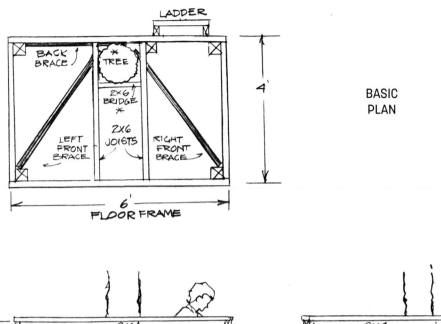

LADDER

BACK BRACE

*TREE

2×6 BRIDGE*

2×6 JOISTS

LEFT FRONT BRACE

RIGHT FRONT BRACE

4'

6' FLOOR FRAME

BASIC PLAN

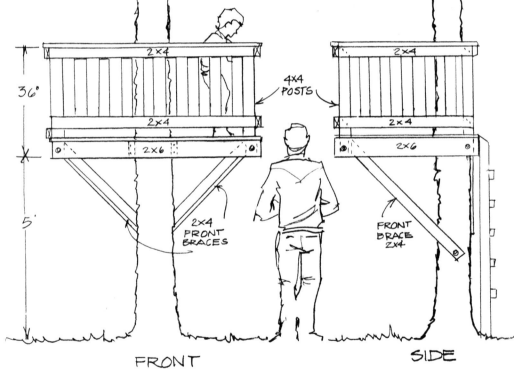

2×4

2×4

2×6

36°

5'

4×4 POSTS

2×4 FRONT BRACES

FRONT

2×4

2×4

2×6

FRONT BRACE 2×4

SIDE

* VARIES AS TO DIAMETER OF TREE

LUMBER

Qty.	Size	Description	Length	Location
(1)	2×4	P.T. lumber	8' long	Rear brace (cut in half)
(1)	2×4	P.T. lumber	12'	Front braces (cut in half)
(2)	2×6	P.T. lumber	10'	Floor frame (cut 6' & 45")
(1)	2×6	P.T. lumber	8 ft.	Floor joists (2 cuts 45")
(1)	¾"	P.T. plywood	4'×8'	Floor (cut off 2 feet to make 4'×6')
(1)	4×4	P.T. lumber	10'	Corner posts (cut into 36")
(1)	4×4	P.T. lumber	6'	Corner posts (cut into 36"
(2)	2×4	P.T. lumber	8'	Side railings (cut into 48")
(2)	2×4	P.T. lumber	10'	Front & rear railings
(1)	⁵⁄₄×6	P.T. lumber	12'	Handrail (cut in half)
(1)	⁵⁄₄×6	P.T. lumber	8'	Handrail (cut in half)
(6)	1×4	P.T. lumber	8'	Vertical slats (cut 24")
(1)	2×4	P.T. lumber	10'	Ladder sides (cut in half)
(1)	2×3	P.T. lumber	8'	Ladder rungs (cut into 18")

HARDWARE

(7)	½"×5"	Galv. lag screws & washers		Braces and rear 2×6 beam to tree and crossbeam
(12)	½"×3"	Galv. lag screws & washers		Floor frame to posts and braces to rear floor frame
(1) 1lb. box	Deck screws	1½"		Plywood floor to frame
(2) 1lb. boxes	Deck screws	3½"		Floor beam corners & railings to corner posts and rungs to ladder

Instructions

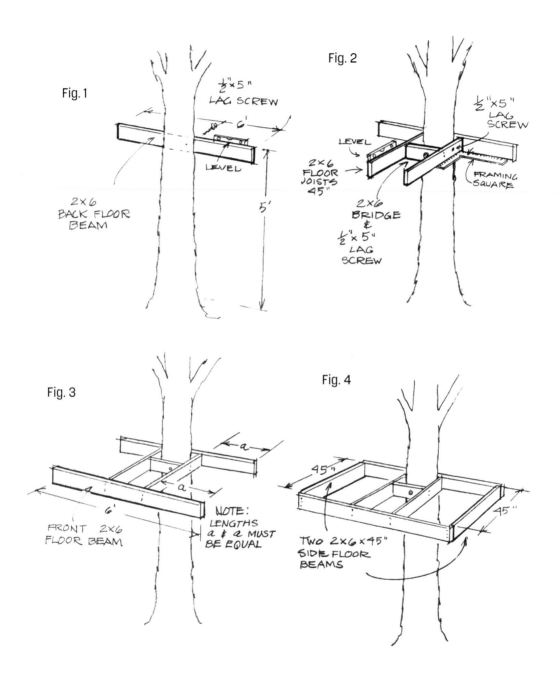

Fig. 1

$\frac{1}{2}" \times 5"$ LAG SCREW

6'

LEVEL

2×6 BACK FLOOR BEAM

5'

Fig. 2

$\frac{1}{2}" \times 5"$ LAG SCREW

LEVEL

2×6 FLOOR JOISTS 45"

2×6 BRIDGE & $\frac{1}{2}" \times 5"$ LAG SCREW

FRAMING SQUARE

Fig. 3

a

a

6'

FRONT 2×6 FLOOR BEAM

NOTE: LENGTHS a & a MUST BE EQUAL

Fig. 4

45"

45"

TWO 2×6×45" SIDE FLOOR BEAMS

Back Floor Beam (2×6)

Cut the 12'-long 2×6 to make two 6' pieces. Take one of the pieces and drill a ½" hole through the middle. **(See Fig. 1).** Insert a ½"×5" lag screw and washer in the hole and hold the board approximately 5 feet up behind the tree. Give the lag screw a rap with a hammer to mark the tree. Using a ⅜" drill, make a pilot hole in the tree. Hold the beam up and hammer the lag screw into the hole. When the screw grips in the hole, switch to a wrench and tighten the lag screw fully. Check for level.

Floor Joists (2×6s)

(See Fig. 2.) Attach a 45"-long 2×6 floor joist to each side of the tree, using a ½"×5" lag screw. Using 3½" deck screws, screw through the back beam into the back end of the joists. Check for level and square. Measure the space between the two joists and cut a piece of 2×6 to fit between them. Screw this bridging piece to the tree using a ½"×5" lag screw and attach to the joists with 3½" deck screws.

Front and Side Beams (2×6s)

Attach the front floor beam to the two joists using 3½" deck screws. Align the front beam to the back beam to ensure that the frame is square. **(See Fig. 3)** Using the two 45" 2×6 side beams, attach each one between the front and back floor beams, using two 3½" screws at each corner. **(See Fig. 4.)**

Plywood Floor (¾"×4'×6')

Cut 2' off the plywood panel to make the 4'×6' floor. Make a cutout 1" bigger than the diameter of the tree. If you have an electric jigsaw, you can make a curve. If not, you can make a square cut using a handsaw. This is easier if you cut the panel in half first. **(See Fig. 15)** Cut 5"× 5" corner notches for the posts. Lift the floor panel onto the deck frame and screw it down using 1½" screws every 6". **(See Figs. 5–7.)**

Railing Posts (4×4s)

Cut five 4×4 posts at 36" each and fit them into the corner holes. Screw them in place, using ½"×3" lag screws. Offset the lag screws so they do not meet in the middle of the post. Each post should be 30" above the floor. **(See Fig. 7 and Fig. 9.)** Note: Depending on which way your tree leans, the

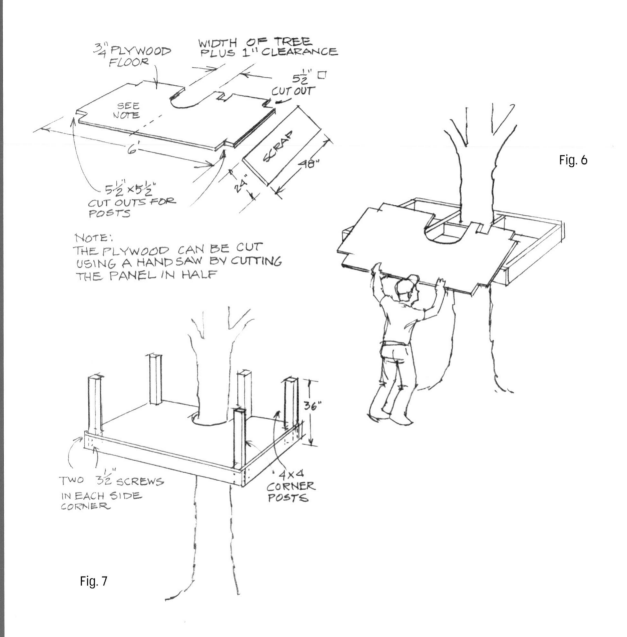

Fig. 5

¾" PLYWOOD FLOOR

WIDTH OF TREE PLUS 1" CLEARANCE

5½" □ CUT OUT

SEE NOTE

SCRAP

6'

48"

24"

5½"x5½" CUT OUTS FOR POSTS

NOTE:
THE PLYWOOD CAN BE CUT USING A HAND SAW BY CUTTING THE PANEL IN HALF

Fig. 6

Fig. 7

36"

TWO 3½" SCREWS IN EACH SIDE CORNER

4x4 CORNER POSTS

railing can be on either side of the tree. If it is on the same side of the tree as the ladder, it will give you an extra post to hold on to while climbing up the ladder.

Front Braces (2×4s)

Cut the 12' 2×4 in half diagonally and hold one piece against the inside of the front corner posts. Mark where the 2×4 brace meets the rear of the tree and cut it off. Screw the brace to the back of the tree using a ½"× 5" lag screw and to the inside front corner post using 3½" screws. **(See Fig. 8 and Fig. 10.)**

Back Brace (2×4)

Cut the 8' 2×4 in half diagonally to make a brace. **(See Fig. 8 and Fig. 11.)** Screw a ½"×5" lag screw through the 2×4 brace and into the tree. You will not need a brace on the other side, because the ladder will support that corner. Note: Since trees almost never grow up in a straight line and aren't perfectly vertical, don't expect this to be a perfect joint. Just make sure that the ends of the braces are well secured to the tree and corner posts. For added strength, drill a 3½" deck screw down through the floor into the brace. **(See Fig. 9.)**

Railings (2×4s)

Each side of the treehouse has two 2×4 railings. The top rail is 30" from the floor, flush with the top of the post, the bottom rail 24" below it. **(See Fig. 12.)** Attach them to the 4×4 corner posts with 3½" deck screws. Cut twenty-two 1×4s into 24" lengths, and, using two 1½" deck screws at each end, attach them 4" apart. Finish off the railing by screwing down a ⅝×6 handrail (ledge). Cut and fit the corners at a 45-degree angle.

Rope Railing

Instead of wooden slats, you might consider weaving ½" rope around the railing. Rope railing is one of our treehouse trademarks. It adds a little to the cost, but gives a much more open "treehouse" feeling that's more in harmony with nature than manufactured pickets bought from the lumber store. Although any rope will do, we recommend using ½" Hempex (available at rwrope.com). Natural colored Hempex looks great and is more durable than most ropes, but is also more expensive. You will need approximately 200' for 4 sides. **(See Fig. 13.)** Allow about 13 feet of rope for each foot of railing length.

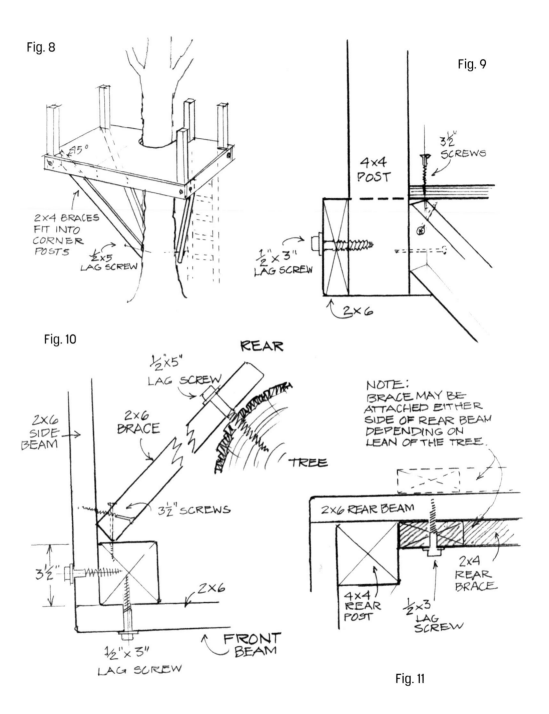

Fig. 8

45°

2×4 BRACES
FIT INTO
CORNER
POSTS

½×5"
LAG SCREW

Fig. 9

3½"
SCREWS

4×4
POST

½"×3"
LAG SCREW

2×6

Fig. 10

REAR

½"×5"
LAG SCREW

2×6
SIDE
BEAM

2×6
BRACE

TREE

3½" SCREWS

3½"

2×6

½"×3"
LAG SCREW

FRONT
BEAM

NOTE:
BRACE MAY BE
ATTACHED EITHER
SIDE OF REAR BEAM
DEPENDING ON
LEAN OF THE TREE.

2×6 REAR BEAM

4×4
REAR
POST

½"×3
LAG
SCREW

2×4
REAR
BRACE

Fig. 11

Fig. 12

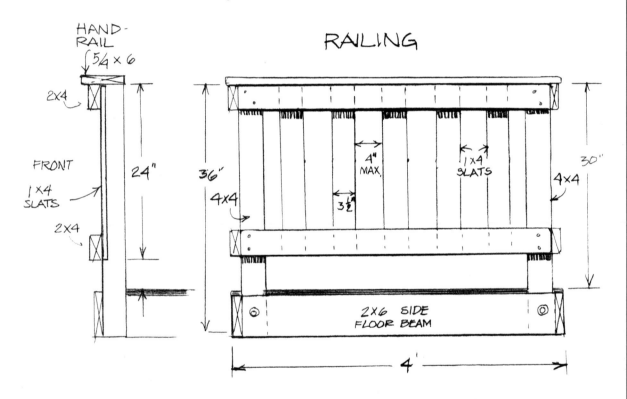

HAND-RAIL
5/4 × 6

2x4

FRONT
1 × 4
SLATS

2x4

24"

RAILING

4"
MAX.

1 × 4
SLATS

3½"

4x4

30"

4x4

36"

4x4

2X6 SIDE
FLOOR BEAM

4'

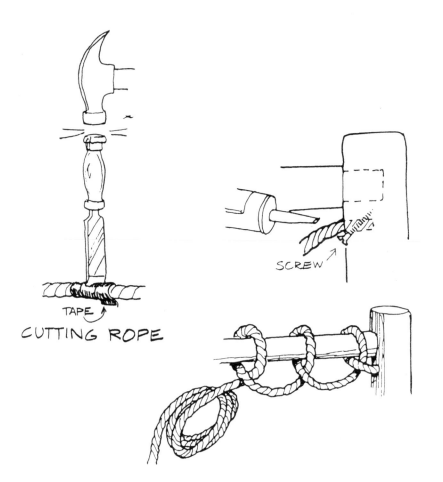

TAPE

CUTTING ROPE

SCREW

Fig. 13

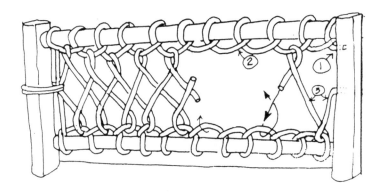

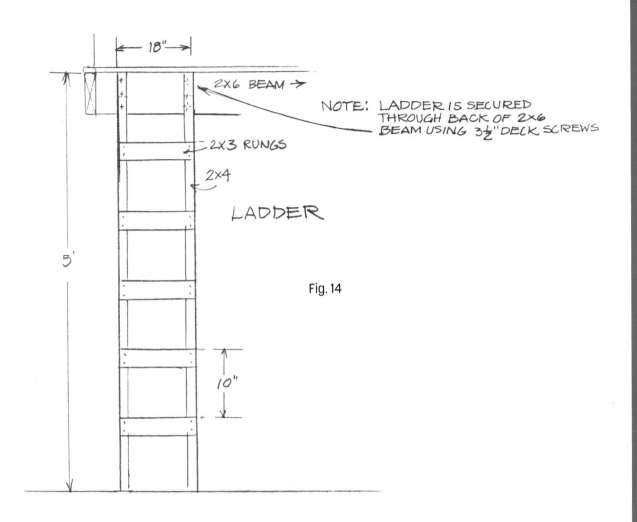

18"

← 2X6 BEAM →

NOTE: LADDER IS SECURED
THROUGH BACK OF 2X6
BEAM USING 3½"DECK SCREWS

2X3 RUNGS

2X4

LADDER

Fig. 14

5'

10"

Fig. 15

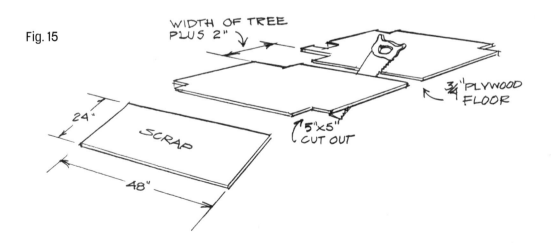

WIDTH OF TREE
PLUS 2"

¾"PLYWOOD
FLOOR

24"

SCRAP

48"

5"X5"
CUT OUT

Begin by boring a ⅝" diameter hole, 1½" deep, into one of the posts just under the top rail. Fill the hole partway with construction adhesive and insert one end of the ½" rope into the hole. Secure the rope with a 2" screw driven at an angle into the rope. The construction adhesive will expand in time, making the joint even tighter.

Feed the rope under and over and "catch" it behind itself before bringing it down and around to form the next loop. Keep the loops about 6" apart on the rail. Continue making loops until you reach the other side, and then secure it as you did the first post. Repeat the same steps on the bottom rail. **(See Fig. 13.)**

To attach the top loops to the bottom loops, begin by boring a ⅝"-diameter hole halfway down the first post, and attach a rope to the post the same way as before. Weave this rope through *every other* loop, making sure to "catch" it behind itself before proceeding. When you reach the second post, drill two ⅝" holes halfway down the post, ⅛" apart, and chisel out the wall between them to form a small pocket for the rope. Insert the rope into the pocket and hold it in place with a screw, then continue back to the opposite post. When you reach the opposite post, drill another ⅝"-diameter hole just beneath the first one and secure it the same way as before.

Tip: The easiest way to cut a rope is to chop it with a large chisel. Seal the end by melting it with a match.

Ladder (2×3s)
Cut the 10' 2×4 in half for the sides of the ladder.

Cut the 10' piece of 2×3 into 18" lengths and screw them to the sides using 3½" deck screws. Attach the ladder to the rear 2×6 deck frame using 3½" screws from the inside. **(See Fig. 14.)**

Using Posts Instead of Braces

Diagonal braces are a good way to support a tree platform, and when you're building high up they are likely to be your best bet. However, if the deck is relatively low to the ground—under 10', say—an alternative is to use vertical posts. This is also a useful option for larger, heavier structures, especially on small trees. Sometimes posts or round poles look more natural than diagonal braces, as they blend in with the tree trunks. They also allow for easier access underneath the platform if you want to hang a swing or hammock there, or simply when it's time to cut the grass.

For the small treehouse described, the two front 4×4 posts in Step #5 can be replaced by longer ones that reach to the ground and below. Measure the distance from the ground to the lowest part of the beam at the front corner—the headroom—then add 6', and round this figure up to the nearest 2'. (Lumber lengths are in 2' increments.) Dig a hole about 30" deep for each of the posts, and make sure they are perfectly aligned as they will double as railing posts. Set the posts using quick-setting concrete, which does not need premixing (but read and follow the instructions on the bag). Attach beams to posts as in step #5. Once the floor is laid, trim the posts to 30" above this level.

KAVITA'S TREEHOUSE

This platform is similar to the one above, but a little bigger—it's 7' wide and 6' deep—and we added a few refinements; it is part of a small aerial village of three treehouses built for a family with three active little boys. (More about connecting treehouses later.)

Because of the greater size and anticipated heavier use of this treehouse, the frame is made of 2×8 pressure-treated beams and joists; the support posts are 6×6, which is perhaps overkill but also part of the chosen look. The posts are also set back from the corners, which makes them less prominent. Every visible edge—posts, beams, ladder, railings—is rounded with a large router bit and carefully sanded to soften the outline and make the whole structure friendly to the touch.

We first established the height of the platform—in this case, as low as possible while still allowing the parents to walk freely underneath—and attached the rear beam to the back of the tree. We used a flexible connection so the tree can continue to grow without harming the treehouse, and you can do the same.

LUMBER

Qty.	Size	Description	Length	Location
2	6×6	P.T. lumber	10' or 12'	Support posts
2	2×8	P.T. lumber	16'	Front & support beams
1	2×8	P.T. lumber	14'	Side beams
3	2×8	P.T. lumber	12'	Joists
4	4×4	Cedar	8'	Railing posts
1	2×6	P.T. lumber	16'	Ladder sides
1	2×4	P.T. lumber	16'	Ladder rungs
1	2×4	Cedar	14'	Railings
3	2×4	Cedar	12'	Railings
8	⁵⁄₄×6	P.T. lumber	14'	Deck boards, top rail
300'	½"	Hempex rope		Rope railing

Instructions

Cut a 2' length of 2×8, beveled at both ends. Bolt it to one face of the rear beam, centered on the middle of the tree trunk. Drill a ½" hole vertically through the sandwiched 2×8s. Thread a ½"×8" shouldered eyebolt through (the eye in line with the beam), and secure with a washer and nut. Hold the beam assembly in place against the tree (eyebolt underneath) and mark through the eye into the bark. Drill a ½" pilot hole, thread a ⁵⁄₈"×10" lag screw and washers through the eye and into the hole, and partially tighten it using a socket wrench. Clamp temporary supports to each end of the beam to hold it horizontal, and tighten the screw further until it is secure but the beam still has some play against the trunk.

Cut two diagonal braces 4' long, with the ends at 45-degree angles. Attach as shown, using 4" lag bolts at the beam and 5" lag screws at the tree. Cut a piece of plywood to reinforce the joint. Fasten with deck screws, and rout the edges smooth. Remove the supports.

As mentioned above, the posts for this design are set in from the corners. They are 5' apart and 5' in front of the rear beam. You can establish the position by dropping a vertical line from the back beam (a piece of wood or a plumb line) and measuring forward from this. The exact position is not critical here, as the floor frame will only rest on the posts and crossbeam. It's okay if you have to move them a little to avoid tree roots, for example. They must, however, be vertical, and their faces aligned with each other.

Dig holes for the two posts, 30" deep or more, and concrete them in. Once they're set firmly, it's time to attach the crossbeam. The *top* of the crossbeam is level with the *bottom* of the rear beam, so the joists can rest on the crossbeam. Mark the posts at this height. Give yourself some wiggle room by using an 8' 2×8 for the crossbeam, and trim it to length once the floor is framed. Clamp it in position, check the levels, and secure with 8" lag bolts through the posts.

For the front corners, this treehouse has an extra detail—the side and front beams each extend 6" (using a cross-halved joint), with an animal head carved on each. The animals—a turtle and fish—were chosen by the kids themselves. We cut the shapes out with a jig-saw and routed the edges. If you do this, make the side beams the lower half of the joint.

The joists are attached with metal joist hangers, at approximately 16" centers. There are also special angle

brackets to attach the perimeter beam—use these at the corners. A larger tree will have some say in spacing the joists, and you may need a bridging piece between those on either side of the trunk, to allow a shorter intermediate joist to fill the gap. With the correct nails, joist hangers are strong, easy to install, and convenient. You can set them in place and simply drop the joists into the pockets, then adjust the angle at the other end so the frame is square. The front beam (the upper part of the cross-halved joint) should just drop onto the sides; use joist hangers where the joists meet the front. We used Simpson Strong-Tie wind ties to fasten the joists to the crossbeam. Instead of plywood we used ⁵⁄₄×6 pressure-treated deck boards for the floor.

The rope railing on this treehouse is different too, and consists of a single continuous rope woven behind itself at every turn. We also set the top rail slightly lower than the posts, so we could fit a horizontal handrail over the rope and railing. It's just a different look.

A platform with deck boards and rope railing inevitably has something of a nautical air, and we played to this theme with our wooden "ratlines" as a fun alternative to the familiar cargo net. Lengths of carefully rounded 2×3 get progressively narrower as they ascend, and are held in place by knotted ropes. Add an impressively antique-looking spyglass from one of the many online sources and your pirates are good to go. It's scientifically proven that sweets hauled up in a bucket taste better than those merely handed up, so a pulley is definitely on the list—attach it to a pole or a rounded 2×2 that's simply screwed to the outside of a railing post. Use a plastic or lightweight wicker basket though, in case someone is walking underneath when it's on the way down. A flagpole is ideal too, and made the same way. Why not design and paint your own flag? We also fitted a "secret message box" to the tree. These touches are for younger kids, of course; but they make the treehouse appeal to a broader age range—your teenagers may be full-on ninjas intent on developing and exercising their athletic powers, but the little ones can use the space in their own way too.

TREE SUMMERHOUSE

This design puts the "house" in "treehouse": it has walls and a roof, a wraparound deck, the indispensable bucket on a pulley for food and supplies, and operable windows with screens to keep out bugs during sleepovers or long summer evenings. It's only lightly enclosed, but the simple cabin makes this a far more versatile structure.

MATERIALS

Qty.	Size	Description	Length	Location
		PLATFORM		
1	2×6	P.T. lumber	10'	V-knee brace
4	2×8	P.T. lumber	10'	Floor frame
7	2×6	P.T. lumber	10'	Floor joists
2	4×4	P.T. lumber	16'	Posts
2	4×4	P.T. lumber	10'	Knee braces & rail posts
2	¾"	AC plywood	4'×8'	Interior floor
7	⁵⁄₄×6	P.T. lumber	10'	Decking
2	2×4	P.T. lumber	10'	Top railing
2	2×4	P.T. lumber	10'	Bottom railing
2	1×2	P.T. lumber	10'	Railing spacers
10	2×2	P.T. lumber	10'	Balusters
		STAIRS		
2	2×6	P.T. lumber	10'	Stringers
1	2×6	P.T. lumber	16'	Treads
		HOUSE		
1	2×4	P.T. lumber	10'	Rear corner posts
4	2×4	P.T. lumber	8'	Sill plates
7	2×4	P.T. lumber	10'	Rear & side wall studs
3	2×4	P.T. lumber	10'	Front wall studs
6	2×4	P.T. lumber	8'	Top plates
2	2×4	P.T. lumber	8'	Front header

Materials list continues on next page.

Qty.	Size	Description	Length	Location
4	2×4	P.T. lumber	8'	Cats
4	3/8"	Lauan ply.	4'×8'	Wall sheathing
6	5/4×4	#2 cedar	10'	Corners & door trim
2	18" bundles	#1 cedar shingles		Walls
GABLED ROOF				
8	2×6	P.T. lumber	12'	Rafters & fascia
1	2×6	P.T. lumber	12'	Ridgepole
20	1×4	P.T. lumber	8'	Nailers
1	2×4	P.T. lumber	12'	Gable frame
1	1×4	P.T. lumber	16'	Trim for insect screen
1	5/4×6	Cedar	14'	Header trim
7	24" bundles	Hand-split cedar shakes		Roofing
1	30-pound roll	Roofing felt		Roof
WINDOWS				
10	1×2	Cedar	12'	Window frames
4	rolls	36" insect screen		Window & gable screens
8	pair	Screen hooks		Screens
8		Screw eyes & hooks		Screens
DOOR				
3	1×6	T&G cedar	10'	Door & battens
2		Wrought-iron strap hinges		
1		Wrought-iron thumb-latch handle		
FASTENERS & HARDWARE				
Nails, lag screws, joist hangers, hinges				
Optional: 1 gallon Cabot gray stain				

Instructions

Fig. 1

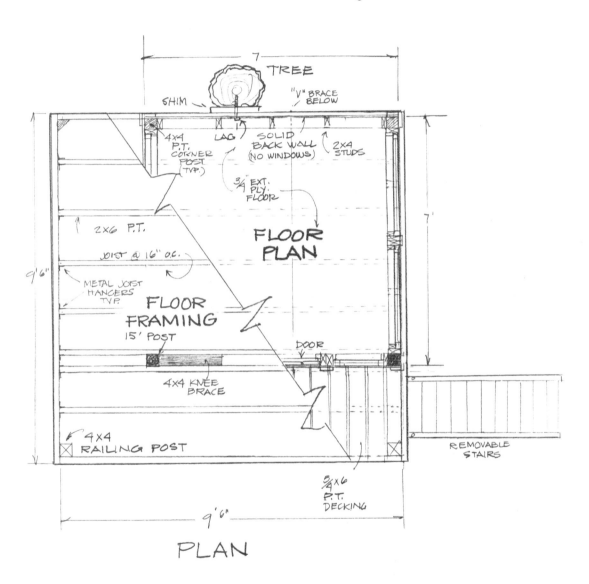

7

TREE

SHIM

"V" BRACE
BELOW

4x4
P.T.
CORNER
POST
(TYP.)

LAG

SOLID
BACK WALL
(NO WINDOWS)

2X4
STUDS

3/4" EXT.
PLY.
FLOOR

FLOOR
PLAN

2X6 P.T.

JOIST @ 16" O.C.

7'

METAL JOIST
HANGERS
TYP.

FLOOR
FRAMING

15' POST

DOOR

9'6"

4X4 KNEE
BRACE

4X4
RAILING POST

REMOVABLE
STAIRS

9'6"

3/4 X 6
P.T.
DECKING

PLAN

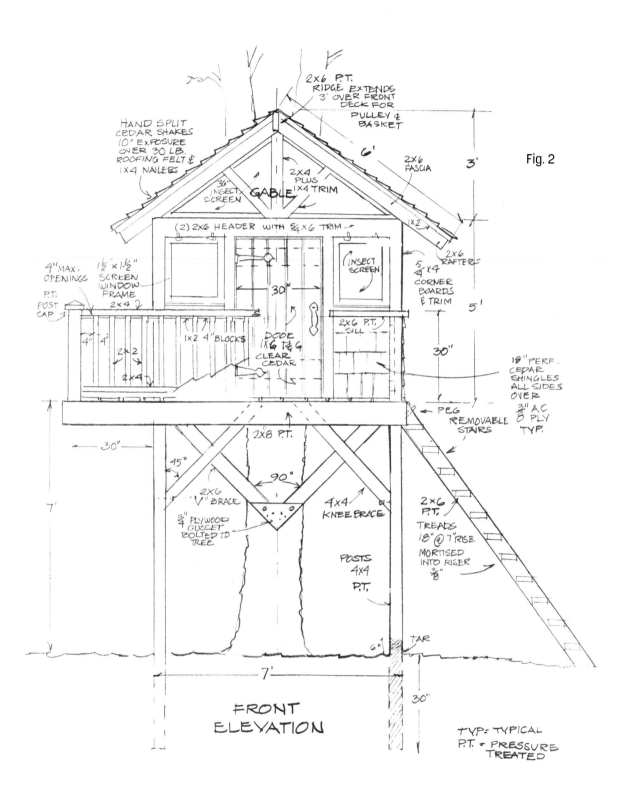

2x6 P.T.
RIDGE EXTENDS
3' OVER FRONT
DECK FOR
PULLEY &
BASKET

HAND SPLIT
CEDAR SHAKES
10" EXPOSURE
OVER 30 LB.
ROOFING FELT &
1x4 NAILERS

2x6
FASCIA

Fig. 2

3'

36"
INSECT
SCREEN

GABLE

2x4
PLUS
1x4 TRIM

6'

1x2

2x6
RAFTERS

(2) 2x6 HEADER WITH 5/4x6 TRIM

4" MAX.
OPENINGS

P.T.
POST
CAP

1½" x 1½"
SCREEN
WINDOW
FRAME
2x4

INSECT
SCREEN

5/4x4
CORNER
BOARDS
& TRIM

5'

30"

4" 4"

2x2

2x4

1x2 4" BLOCKS

30"

DOOR
1x6 T&G
CLEAR
CEDAR

2x6 P.T.
SILL

30"

18" PERF.
CEDAR
SHINGLES
ALL SIDES
OVER
¾" A.C.
5 PLY
TYP.

PEG
REMOVABLE
STAIRS

2x8 P.T.

45°

90°

2x6
"V" BRACE

¾" PLYWOOD
GUSSET
BOLTED TO
TREE

4x4
KNEE BRACE

2x6
P.T.
TREADS
18" @ 7" RISE
MORTISED
INTO RISER
⅜"

7'

POSTS
4x4
P.T.

6"

TAR

7'

30"

FRONT
ELEVATION

TYP = TYPICAL
P.T. = PRESSURE
TREATED

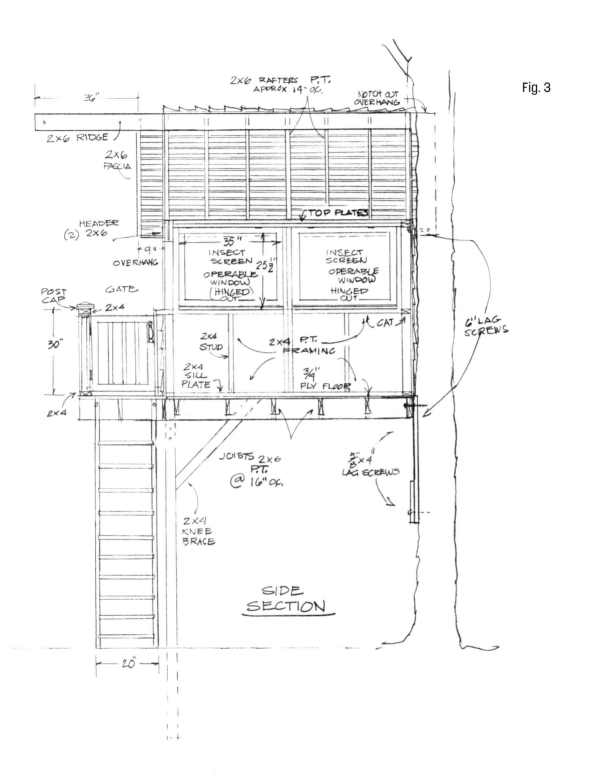

Fig. 3

2X6 RAFTERS P.T.
APPROX 14" O.C.

NOTCH OUT
OVERHANG

36"

2X6 RIDGE

2X6
FASCIA

TOP PLATES

HEADER
(2) 2X6

35"
INSECT
SCREEN
OPERABLE
WINDOW
(HINGED
OUT

INSECT
SCREEN
OPERABLE
WINDOW
HINGED
OUT

25½"

9"
OVERHANG

POST
CAP

GATE

2X4

CAT

6" LAG
SCREWS

30"

2X4
STUD

2X4 P.T.
FRAMING

2X4
SILL
PLATE

¾"
PLY FLOOR

2X4

JOISTS 2X6
P.T.
@ 16" O.C.

⅜" X 4
LAG SCREWS

2X4
KNEE
BRACE

SIDE
SECTION

20"

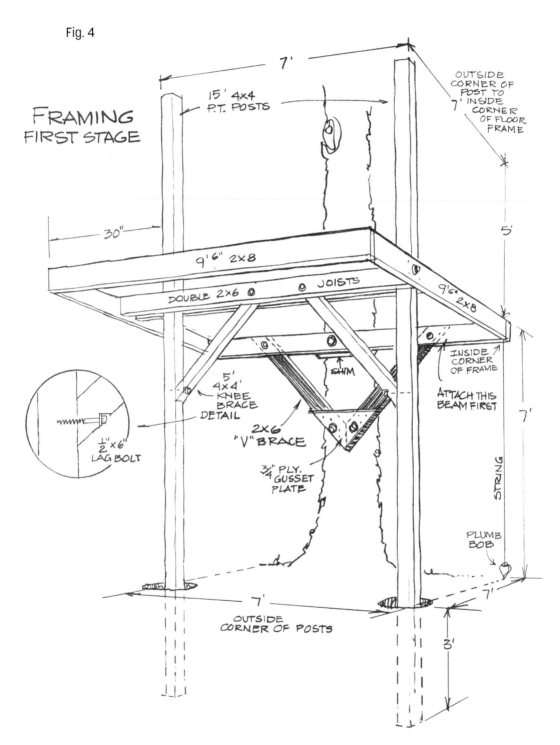

Fig. 4

FRAMING
FIRST STAGE

7'

15' 4x4
P.T. POSTS

OUTSIDE
CORNER OF
POST TO
INSIDE
7' CORNER
OF FLOOR
FRAME

30"

5'

9'6" 2x8

DOUBLE 2x6   JOISTS

9'6" 2x8

INSIDE
CORNER
OF FRAME

SHIM

5'
4x4
KNEE
BRACE
DETAIL

ATTACH THIS
BEAM FIRST

2x6
"V" BRACE

1/2"x6"
LAG BOLT

3/4" PLY.
GUSSET
PLATE

STRING

7'

PLUMB
BOB

OUTSIDE
CORNER OF POSTS

7'

7'

3'

Start with the rear beam. Cut a 9'6" length of 2×8 and attach it to the front of the tree at the desired height as described above; a large, mature tree may not require a flexible connection, and can simply be fastened with a ⅝"×8" lag screw and washer. Shim as necessary between beam and tree so the face of the beam is vertical. **(See Fig. 1 and Fig. 4.)** Make sure the beam is horizontal before final tightening.

Cut two 5' braces, with the ends at an angle of 45 degrees. Make a gusset plate out of ¾" plywood and attach to the bottom of the "V." Bolt the braces to the beam, and secure to the tree trunk with lag screws. **(See Fig. 2 and Fig. 4.)**

Drop a plumb line off one end of the beam to the ground; measure 7' forward from this point to mark the position of the first post. For the second post, measure 7' across from the first post and 7' forward from the back beam. Using spare lengths of lumber laid on the ground, check that the diagonals are equal, and adjust until they are—the posts will form the front corners of the treehouse as well as supporting the platform, and must be placed accurately. Dig the two 3' holes and drop the posts into them. Do not backfill the holes with concrete until you have built the floor frame—this will allow you to adjust the posts if necessary. You can hold them temporarily in place with three diagonal braces made from scraps of wood.

Attach the front and side 2×8 perimeter beams to the posts, and use metal joist hangers for the intermediate 2×6 joists—note that the posts are sandwiched between two joists. Double-check the angles of the frame and the posts, and fill the holes with concrete. Cut two 5'-long 4×4 braces with 45-degree angles at the ends. Secure to the post with a 6"×½" lag screw and to the joists with an 8"×½" bolt.

Cut two pieces of ¾" exterior plywood for the interior floor, each 42"×7', and fasten to the deck frame with 2½" deck screws. Use ⁵⁄₄×6 pressure-treated boards for the outside deck.

Frame the walls with 2×4s **(see Fig. 3),** using a single 2×4 sill plate at the bottom and a double 2×4 plate at the top; for the front wall, use a double 2×6 header.

Frame the roof with 2×6 rafters. Fasten them to the wall plates using wind-ties, and screw the tops to an 11' 2×6 ridge beam. The beam extends out over the front deck to provide an attachment for the indispensable pulley and basket.

Allow a 9" roof overhang at the front of the treehouse. Attach 1×4 nailers at 10" centers. Cut and fit fascias, decorative gable details, and trim. Cover the nailers with roofing felt and 24" hand-split cedar shakes. (See instructions on product packages.)

WINDOW SCREEN

EXTERIOR

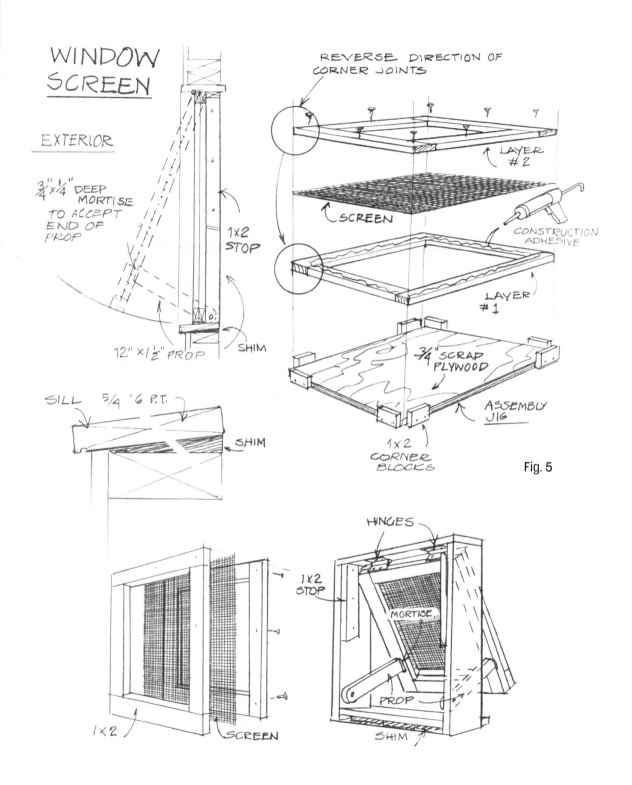

$\frac{3}{4}" \times \frac{1}{4}"$ DEEP MORTISE TO ACCEPT END OF PROP

1x2 STOP

12" X 1½" PROP

SHIM

SILL   5/4 '6 P.T.

SHIM

REVERSE DIRECTION OF CORNER JOINTS

LAYER #2

SCREEN

CONSTRUCTION ADHESIVE

LAYER #1

¾" SCRAP PLYWOOD

ASSEMBLY JIG

1x2 CORNER BLOCKS

Fig. 5

HINGES

1x2 STOP

MORTISE

PROP

SHIM

1x2

SCREEN

The walls are ⅜" AC plywood covered with 18" cedar shingles. Be careful that the points of the shingling nails don't protrude through the plywood, unless you intend to panel the inside walls. Alternatively, use construction adhesive and ⅝" staples to attach the shingles.

Make the 30"-wide door out of 1×6 T&G cedar boards screwed to a horizontal ledge (batten) at top and bottom. **(See Fig. 2.)**

The screened windows can be fixed or hinged. You can easily make multiple windows with a simple jig. **(See Fig. 5.)** Cut a scrap of plywood to the size of the window opening (minus ⅛" on each side for clearance). Nail short pieces of 1×2 to the corners as shown to hold the layers in place while you assemble them. Cut pieces of 1×2 to fit neatly into the corner blocks. Apply construction adhesive to the joints and the top of the first layer of 1×2s. Cut a piece of screen to the size of the window and place it on top of the first layer. Cut pieces of 1×2 for the top layer making sure they overlap the bottom layer at the corners. **(See Fig. 5.)** Screw the layers together using 1¼" coated screws.

Cut a triangle of insect screen to fit the gable; staple it to the inside of the joists and decorative trim. Cut and attach pieces of 1×2 to cover and seal the inside edges.

Make the stairs out of 2×6 treads, mortised or just securely screwed into 2×6 risers.

Paint or stain the treehouse as desired. For a decorative touch, pick out the trim in an accent color. Alternatively, use clear acrylic varnish to preserve the new-wood look, or simply let it weather to an unobtrusive gray.

ALL-SEASON TREEHOUSE

This treehouse takes the same game plan a step further. Bigger than those described above, it's made from heavier lumber to be extra sturdy and to match the style of the adventure course alongside it; every edge has been rounded, routed, and sanded to please the eye and hand. It is fully enclosed, has hinged glazed windows with trim, a Dutch door, wraparound deck, and staircase with handrails. The design is ideal for the teenage ninja owners and for their hospitable parents. It could easily be wired for electricity to extend its use into four seasons, although that was not required in this case.

AS-1

MATERIALS

Qty.	Size	Description	Length	Location
2	6×6	P.T. lumber	16'	Support posts
2	6×6	P.T. lumber	8'	Rear corner posts
5	4×4	P.T. lumber	8'	Braces, bottom stair posts
1	4×4	P.T. lumber	10'	Braces
5	4×4	Cedar	8'	Railing posts
1	2×8	P.T. lumber	16'	Door and window headers
18	2×8	P.T. lumber	14'	Floor supports and joists
3	2×8	P.T. lumber	10'	Ridge beam, stair treads
2	2×6	P.T. lumber	10'	Stair stringers
10	2×6	P.T. lumber	8'	Rafters
20	2×4	P.T. lumber	16'	Framing
8	2×4	Cedar	14'	Railings
22	2×2	Cedar	8'	Railing spindles
27	⁵⁄₄×6	P.T. lumber	14'	Deck boards
2	½"	Exterior plywood	4'×8'	Cabin floor
2	⁵⁄₄×6	P.T. lumber	10'	Stair handrails
4	⁵⁄₄×6	Cedar	14'	Deck handrail
4	1×8	Cedar	14'	Deck edge trim
560	1×6	Cedar T&G	LF	Wall sheathing
5	1×6	Cedar	10'	Eaves, door
11	1×6	Cedar	8'	Trim: rafters, door, and windows
8	1×4	Cedar	10'	Trim: corners, door, and windows
4	1×4	Cedar	8'	Walls: base trim
4	1×3	Cedar	8'	Corner trim
1	¼"	Plexiglas	4'×8'	Gable window
2	31"×29"	Barn sashes		Windows
5	1×2	Cedar	12'	Draught strip, door edges
50	3'×50' roll	Roofing felt		Roof
5	Bundles	Asphalt shingles		Roof covering

Instructions

All trees come out of the tree factory different from all the others, and that's how we like it. Even a treehouse with a relatively straightforward connection to the host tree must deal with this simple fact. Most important is to have a tree that's big and sturdy enough to support the rear beam and to look "right" doing so—you can always add support with extra posts and braces but the tree was there first and must be happy with its guest. Our chosen tree has a broad trunk that separates into three above the level of the deck but below the roof, giving the structure both a firm anchor and visual interest. The platform did not have to be very high off the ground, so we were able to have the support posts reach all the way to the top of the walls.

The first step is to determine the height and orientation of the rear beam, which immediately establishes exactly where the treehouse will go and which direction it will face. Our tree's gradually diverging trunk gave us two natural points of connection for the beam, and by trying it at different heights we were able to adjust the angle until it looked right. A 14' 2×8 is potentially cumbersome, but with two lifters and a "spotter" it's manageable. We marked the beam at the two points where it touched the tree, and drilled ⅝" holes at these points. Marking the tree through the holes (making sure the beam was level), we drilled ½" pilot holes. The trunk was quite vertical at our chosen spot; otherwise we would have shimmed the beam as necessary to keep it from tilting forward or back. It's attached with ⅝"×8" lag screws; for stability, we then "sistered" it with another 2×8 beam, secured with screws. There are also two diagonal 4×4 braces running from the beam to the foot of the tree. We found natural "pockets" among the roots to anchor them, but if the platform had been higher we'd have fixed them to the trunk. The tops of the braces have shoulder joints and are held by 4" lag screws.

The 6×6 support posts for the cantilevered deck were also to form the front corners of the treehouse, and therefore had to be placed precisely. The cabin was to be 8'×8', so the posts would be 8' apart (outside to outside). Our original design would have put the back wall flush with the rear beam, but the tree had other ideas, as the diverging trunks were leaning out over the deck. We decided to bring the house forward by about 18" and deepen the whole platform accordingly, to make the front deck as generous as the sides while keeping the rear wall and roof clear of the tree. This worked out well, as we ended up with an extra, "secret" rear deck only accessible to kids and the narrower kind of adult (including ourselves, fortunately). You can design a treehouse but must submit your ideas for the tree's consideration. The outcome of this was that the posts would be 8' apart but 9'6" from the rear beam. You are unlikely to face exactly the same situation, but this shows the importance of assessing the situation and working with the tree; adapting is fun and often leads to a more interesting result.

The support posts are 16' pressure-treated 6×6s, the longest we could obtain locally on this occasion; they were just long enough to reach the top of the walls—if the platform had been any higher we would have built the cabin separately after the deck boards were in place. Given the size and weight of these posts, it was easier to secure the first one permanently and build the rest of the structure with that as the reference point.

Locate the middle of the rear beam, and from this point measure and mark 4' in either direction. These two points represent the outer sides of the cabin frame. Clamp a long straight piece of wood to the beam at each mark so that it reaches the ground, and adjust until it is vertical in both directions. Clamp or temporarily screw a length of wood across these pieces at the base. Lay another length of wood on the ground at right angles to it at the vertical mark. Measure 9'6" along this line and dig a 3'-deep posthole; drop the post into the hole and brace temporarily. Double-check and adjust distance and angles, making sure the post is perfectly plumb and its face square to the wood on the ground. Use quick-setting concrete to secure the post. It's a good habit to keep checking the angles as you fill the hole, because you won't get another chance once it's set.

Use the same method to establish the position of the second post. Dig the hole, drop the post in, and brace it while you make final adjustments. It should be 8' (outside to outside) from the first post, 9'6" from the back beam, square to the wood on the ground and to the first post, with equal corner-to-corner diagonals, and vertical. (Well done!) It's almost impossible to match the heights of the two posts—easier just to trim as necessary later. Concrete the post in, and the groundwork is finished.

The crossbeam consists of twin 14' 2×8s bolted across the support posts, with the posts sandwiched between them. Because the deck is cantilevered, the 2×8 floor joists rest on the crossbeam, so the *top* of the crossbeam must be level with the *bottom* of the rear beam; run a straight piece of wood and a level between rear beam and post to find this height, and mark the posts. Use the wood and a square to ensure that the ends of the crossbeam are in the right place to support the two side perimeter beams. Clamp the twin beams in position, and secure with two ⅝"×10" carriage bolts per post.

The deck is 13' deep; allowing for the thickness of the front beam and sistered rear beam, the joists will be 12'7½" long. Like the crossbeam, the joists are doubled at the posts. Fit the two sides and the front beam first (making sure the frame is square), then the intermediates. Use joist hangers to attach them to the front and rear beams, and wind ties at the crossbeam. At the posts, use carriage bolts as above. (Make a habit of checking these, and all other bolts, several times during construction—they can work surprisingly loose while you're not looking.)

Cut four identical lengths of 4×4, 4' long with 45-degree angles at each end, to brace the posts and crossbeam. Attach them to the posts with countersunk ½"×6" lag screws, and between the two parts of the crossbeam with ½"×10" carriage bolts. Use short lengths of ¾×6 decking as spacers between braces and beams. Fit a third brace to the front face of each post; this will need to be longer than the others, as its top end runs up between two joists—cut the bottom angle on a 5' 4×4 and test-fit in place, marking the required length against the top of the joist. Attach as before. **(See photo AS-2.)**

AS-2

The posts for the deck railing are 4×4 cedar, 43¼" long; secure them to the inside of the perimeter beams, flush with the bottom, using three 3½" timber screws. At the corners of the deck, insert screws from both faces. Install a post in the middle of each face, and another near the corner where the stairs will go; this will form the second newel post for the stairs—place it to leave an opening 2' wide. Because our tree leaned inward above the deck, we stopped the railing, with an additional post, either side of the trunk, to give the tree room to grow. It's better not to build the railing itself yet, since there'll be a lot of material to lift up onto the deck during construction. As a safety measure, attach a temporary top rail of 2×4s to remind everyone where the edge of the deck is—it can easily be removed for access.

The deck boards are ⅝×6, spaced for drainage. Set out several of them more or less in the right position; this will make it easier to move around until you've actually installed a section of deck. Choose a straight board to start at the front edge; you'll need to notch it to fit around the posts. Fasten with two 2½" deck screws at every joist. The screws should be 1¼" from the edge of the board. Use a pencil, screwdriver, or other object of suitable thickness to space the next board evenly from the first. Some boards may need persuading into a straight line with some gentle leverage—sometimes you can just stand on the board and tap it into line with your heel, then secure it with a screw.

Continue in the same way, periodically checking that the boards are still parallel to front and rear beams—they can tend to fan out in one or other direction if you're not careful, which would make the last section difficult and untidy. When you get halfway, you will have to cut the boards to fit the intermediate posts, which may leave a board unsupported at the end. In this case, attach a block of 2×4 to the inside of the post underneath. If you are lucky, the boards will reach the back of the deck and fit flush to the edge; check this by setting out the last few before screwing them down—you may be able to steal or lose a little by altering the spacing fractionally. Deck boards are also available in 4" width, and you can use one or more of these.

If neither of these options is possible, rip the last board to size and rout the edge to match the others.

Trim the supporting posts to the height of the sidewalls. Ours are 7' above deck level, which is quite tall for a treehouse, but this also had to accommodate some large adults. The black Teflon-coated Bahco Superior saw is good for this—it cuts smoothly even through pressure-treated wood. Mark all four sides using a square. Cut a shallow groove in one side, then gradually angle the heel of the saw into the adjacent side, making sure the cut follows both lines; once it is "biting" you can angle the tip of the saw into the opposite side in the same way. By alternating angles you can feel your way across the post; let the saw do the work, and the fourth side will be straight if the others are. Use a level to find the same height on the second post. Mark and cut them. Cut two more 6×6s to 7' long. These are the rear corners of the walls.

The wall frames are made from 2×4s, with headers of doubled 2×8s over the windows and door. Start with a sidewall.

Cut two 2×4s to 85"; these are the top and bottom plates. Mark the midpoint of each. The vertical studs are 81"—their bases will rest on the bottom plates and the top plates will rest in turn on them; cut four.

Lay the top, bottom, and outer studs out on the deck, and join the corners, using two nails or screws per joint and making sure the corners are square.

For windows we used ready-made barn sashes from www.menards.com. Our chosen size was 31" wide x 29" high. The rough opening in the walls is 2" wider and 2½" taller (to allow for trim all round and sill underneath), which comes to 33" wide x 31½" high. Measure 16½" either side of the middle mark on the plates. This is the inside face of the stud. Nail to the bottom plate, check for square and fix to the top plate. Cut a 2×4 to 33" long and attach it between the studs 36" above the base of the bottom plate, making sure this too is square—it's called a rough opening but the more accurate it is, the easier it will be to fit the window and decorative trim. Cut three 2×4s each 27" long, to support the bottom of the window at the ends and middle; nail in place. Cut two 2×8s each 33" long, and attach them side by side on edge at the top of the window opening—31" above the sill.

AS-3

Lift the wall frame to butt against the front corner post, with their outer faces flush. Clamp it in place and check that all angles are still square. Screw the frame to the post at top, bottom, and three intermediate points. Don't fix it to the deck yet, but place a temporary brace at the other end just in case. **(See photo AS-3.)**

Build the other sidewall in the same way, and fix to the corresponding post.

The rear wall has no window, so there are three equidistant studs between the sides. Cut two 2×4s to 85" and five to 81". Join these together as before.

AS-4

Lift one of the 6×6 7'-long rear corner posts into position, and attach the end of the sidewall to it. Attach the rear wall at right angles to the side. Join the other post to the remaining side and to the rear wall. Check for square at the corners. At this stage only the front posts are fixed, so the other corners can if necessary be judiciously persuaded into alignment. Once you're happy with it, screw the frame to the deck, beginning with the rear wall: locate one of the joists, so you can fasten right through into it. Attach the frame at several points. On the sidewalls, angle the screws outward so that their points go into the joists that run along the outside of the support posts.

The front frame has four 81"-long 2×4 studs; the top and bottom plates are 85" long. For the rough opening of the doorway, cut two 2×4s each to 73" and two 2×8s to 35". **(See photo AS-4.)**

Mark the middle of the plates, and join the outer studs to both. Measure 17½" either side of the middle mark, and attach the intermediate studs with their inner faces at this distance. Attach the two 73" studs to the inner faces of these studs, flush with the bases. Carefully cut out the middle (doorway) section of the bottom plate——a separate sill will be added later.

Lift the frame and attach to the support posts and deck. Check all angles, and add the 2×8 double header over the doorway.

Cut two 2×4s to 8' long, to form a second top plate for the front and rear wall frames; attach them to the top plate and corner posts. Cut and fit two more to 7'5" long for the sidewalls.

Cut and fit two pieces of ½" plywood for the cabin floor. Mark the positions of the deck joists onto the bottom plate first, so you can transfer these to the plywood and secure it without nails poking through under the deck.

We prefer to clad the sidewalls before fitting the rafters, as it's simpler. Here we used rough cedar V-joint tongue andand groove for a finished but not too fussy look. The boards fit flush to the corners of the wall, which should be a span of exactly 8'. Set the first board at the base of the wall, with the central tongue facing upward. Using 2" annular stainless-steel nails, fix it to the bottom plate at several points. At each stud, drive another nail through the shoulder of the tongue, angling it downward at 45 degrees. Drive the head of the nail flush with the shoulder using a suitably sized nail punch, being careful not to split the tongue. Unless you have just lost your nail punch in leaf litter and are a hundred miles from civilization, try to resist the temptation to use a large blunted nail for this: the metal is too soft and sooner or later will skid off and cause damage to wood or woodworker.

The groove of the second board fits over the tongue of the first, and you therefore only need to nail through the tongue for this and subsequent courses—secret nailing. Make sure the groove is fully seated. If necessary, place a short scrap of tongue-and-groove board (with the tongue removed) over any stubborn spots and tap it gently with a mallet. In this way, work your way up the sides, trimming the boards to fit around the window opening. Finish at the top plate, or wherever the next whole board reaches above it. Repeat with the opposite sidewall.

AS-5

If the top board extends above the plate, carefully cut out a notch 1½" wide at each end, down to the level of the top plate, so that the weight of the roof joists will be taken by the plate rather than the cedar cladding. Cut another notch at the midpoint of the board, and another at each quarter—there will be five rafters per side.

The pitch and overhang of the roof have a big influence on the overall look and balance of the whole building, so we often leave the fine-tuning of this till the walls are up. Here's how . . .

From the front deck, measure and mark the exact center of the front wall top plate, and make a second mark ¾" to the right of it. Take a straight length of wood (a 12' 2×4 would be ideal) and stand it upright so that its left edge is flush with the second (off-center) mark. Clamp it in place and adjust till it's perfectly vertical and aligned. Place a similar "mast" at the back wall, making sure to offset it to the same side by ¾".

Take an 8' length of 2×6 (the first rafter) and rest the lower edge in the notch at the front of the right-hand wall; you can then move the top end to try out variations of overhang and pitch—simply clamp the 2×6 to the mast in different places until you're happy with it. Mark the top cut for the rafter using the left side of the mast as a guide, and mark the mast at the top of the rafter. At the rafter tail, mark the vertical up from the point where the rafter touches the outside of the wall; 2" from the bottom of this line, mark a line at right angles to it for the seat of the triangular "bird's-mouth" notch that will rest on the wall plate. Cut the rafter and set it aside. **(See photo AS-5.)**

The ridge beam is a 2×8, 10' long. This gives a generous overhang for the front gable and a few inches at the back, where the leaning tree left a smaller space. Clamp the beam to the left side of the masts at the height you marked from the rafter, making sure it's horizontal. Try the rafter at all four corners of the roof—it should fit all of them. Using this rafter as the master copy, mark and cut nine more.

Using a level, mark a vertical line on the ridge beam flush with the outside of the top plate; this marks the outside of the front rafters. Set the first rafter on the top plate and secure to the beam with a screw angled down into the beam. Put a long timber screw through the throat of the bird's-mouth notch into the double top plate, and add a wind tie for good measure. Repeat for the other rafters. Remove the temporary masts.

The front and rear walls are clad with cedar tongue and groove, cut flush with the ends of the sidewalls. For the front wall, which has a triangular window filling the gable, leave the second top plate uncovered, forming a recess where the window will fit. The rear wall is clad right to the ridge. Above the top plates, install vertical 2×4s

AS-6

first, to continue the studs up to the rear rafters, toenailing them to the top plates and with shoulder joints at the top. At the gable, cut the cedar cladding overlong, and trim the boards afterward with a sharp saw, using the rear rafters as a guide. You'll need to notch the boards to fit around the protruding ridge beam. **(See photo AS-6.)**

To build the sidewalls up to the top of the rafters, cut small pieces of 1×2 and attach them vertically to the sides of the rafters, flush with the outside of the frame. Cut and fit sections of tongue and groove to these pieces, trimming as necessary at the top so that the roof will close the gap. (You can also run a bead of caulk along this joint later.)

The roof is made of the same cedar boards, with the V-groove on the underside—the tree-house ceiling. Secret nailing confers no particular advantage here, since the roof is going to be shingled, but it's still a good idea to have the tongues uppermost. Cut the boards to overhang the ridge beam by 1½" at each end. Matching the two sides of the roof at the ridge may be easier if you work down from the top, surface-nailing or using deck screws as you go. This also means you can work from a stepladder inside the building for the upper sections, but be careful not to put your foot through the vulnerable sections of wall between the rafters. Let the bottom roof board extend an inch beyond the rafter tails.

Cut and fit 2×4s on edge to the underside of the gables, flush with the ends of the roof boards. Fit aluminum drip strips to the edges of the roof.

Cover the entire roof with roofing felt—we used the self-adhesive kind. Follow the instructions on the packaging, and overlap the roof edges by an inch or so. Our 2×4 temporary deck rail made a useful scaffolding for this part of the job, but to fit the ridge section you'll probably have to perch like a cowboy on a wide but bony horse—fortunately, in the right footwear and dry weather, the felt gives a lot more traction than wooden boards. **(See photo AS-7.)**

AS-7

The roof is finished with standard asphalt shingles (we picked a soft shade of bark brown that goes well with the setting and design). Again, follow the manufacturer's advice on installation. The ridge has a cedar cap made from a 1×3 and a 1×4 joined at the appropriate angle (formed by ripping one edge of each board). We glued and screwed the two pieces together, then attached them to the roof as a unit.

The deck railings are made from cedar 2×4s and 2×2s. First make a simple "story stick" from a piece of 1×2 a few inches longer than the longest run of railing (from one post to the next). Mark the stick every 5" along one narrow side, and again 1½" beyond each mark. Use a square to extend the marks across the side. This gives the position of the 1½" spindles and the 3½" gaps between them.

Measure the distance between two posts and cut a top and bottom rail to fit exactly between them. Align them side by side on the deck, and adjust the story board so that the space between the last spindle and the post will be the same at both ends; transfer the marks to both rails.

Cut the spindles to 29". Lay a length of ⁵⁄₄×6 deck board along the base of the treehouse wall, and another parallel to it 29" from the wall. Place the spindles at right angles to the wall on top of the boards, and stand the top rail on edge beside the outer board. This will center the spindle on the rail. Line up the spindle with the marks on the rail, and attach the first spindle with a deck screw through the rail, making sure they're at right angles. Doing it this way makes it quite easy for one person to do quickly and accurately on-site. It's a good idea to attach the two end spindles first, so the rail is braced against the wall while you fit the intermediates. Once you've done the top rail, turn the assembly so the rail is now braced against the wall, and slide the inner ⁵⁄₄×6 from under it—otherwise the spindles won't be lying horizontally—and attach the bottom rail the same way.

AS-8

AS-9

The railing can be fixed with pocket holes, for which there are special jigs to guide the drill; alternatively you can (with care) drill a diagonal pilot hole in the rail using a normal power drill: slowly and gently start a hole at right angles to the surface, and as soon as the bit begins to cut, tilt the drill toward the end of the rail. This may require a little practice on scrap wood, and you can expect to break one or two thin drill bits as a reward for enthusiasm. Drill the top rail from above, as the screw will be covered by the handrail. Ideally the bottom rail should be fixed from below, if you have a flexible extension for the drill. The top rail finishes flush with the top of the posts. A suitable piece of scrap wood underneath each end will make this easier to arrange.

AS-10

Work your way round, making all the railings the same way. **(See photos AS-8 and AS-9.)**

The deck is faced all round with 1×8 cedar to match the railings and walls. Simply cut to size and nail or screw flush with the top of the deck. This leaves a narrow shadow-line under the cedar trim, for a nice little detail.

The stairs are made of pressure-treated wood—2×6 stringers, and 2×8 treads 21" across. We thought a ladder would be too basic for this more elaborate design. The deck was about 80" above the ground (depending on where it was measured from). We made the angle a relaxed 50(-ish) degrees, so the owners could easily step, rather than climb, up and down. It was a rather untechnical matter of propping a 10' length of 2×6 against the deck and adjusting it until it looked and felt right. We marked and cut the vertical at the top, and cut the bottoms to rest on the uneven ground 21" apart. One stringer had to be longer than the other and slightly sculpted to fit the space. We could have set the ends on blocks or a cast concrete slab, but in this case preferred to work around the dense network of exposed tree roots. **(See photo AS-10.)**

The treads have a rise of 8", which meant there would be ten steps including the deck. The positions can be marked by using a framing square and a pair of stair gauges (small brass clamps that attach to the square and make repeat measurements quick and accurate). From the top inside of the stringer, measure 8" down the cut vertical line and place the heel of the square at this point. Mark the horizontal to the top edge of the stringer. This line indicates the top of the tread. Attach the stair gauges to the two sides (blade and tongue) of the square to maintain the angle against the edge. Slide the square down the stringer until the heel is

8" below the marked horizontal, and mark the next step. Continue to the end, and repeat for the other stringer.

Attach the treads to the first stringer, using three 3½" timber screws for each. Make sure the treads are square to the stringer and aligned with each other: one rogue step sticking out half an inch can be dangerous to the unwary user. Attach the second stringer, lift the stairs into place and fasten to the rear beam with timber screws, centrally positioned between the newel posts on the deck.

The staircase has a handrail on each side, mounted on 4×4 posts at the foot; here again, we chose not to disturb the tree roots by digging, but simply attached the posts firmly to the outside of the stringers with timber screws. The handrail is supported by a 2×4 rail on edge. This fits flush with the top of the post, with the ⁵⁄₄×6 handrail on top. Take extra care rounding and sanding the handrail so there won't be any nasty surprises. **(See photo AS-11.)**

The deck railing has a similar handrail, made of cedar. The mitered corners may take a little finagling; we like to cut all the pieces and clamp them into place, making any necessary minor adjustments before fixing them permanently. **(See photo AS-12.)**

The front gable features a large triangular fixed window of Plexiglas. To brace it in the middle, we first attached a 2×4 on edge between the wall plate and ridge beam. **(See photo AS-13.)**

The Plexiglas is supported around its edge by the top plate and rafters; it should overlap these by 1". Measure and mark the sheet, and cut to size using a circular saw with a carbide-tipped blade. It's important to get the blade up to full speed before starting the

AS-11

AS-12

cut; if in doubt, practice on a spare piece of Plexiglas. You will need to cut a small notch at the top, where the window meets the ridge beam. Use a jigsaw with the appropriate blade. Put a bead of silicone around the top plate and rafters and lift the window into place; temporarily secure it with plastic-headed roofing nails.

Cut two lengths of cedar 1×6 to cover the rafters, and attach them with annular nails. Be careful not to nail through the Plexiglas, which will crack if you do. Cut and fit a 1×4 to cover the bottom of the window.

A vertical 1×3 covers the middle brace on the outside. Cut and notch out to fit. Drill three narrow pilot holes down the center, and mark the corresponding positions on the window. Drill oversize holes in the Plexiglas (there are specialized drill bits for this), and screw the 1×3 into place. We fitted two further pieces of 1×3 trim, as shown. These are simply glued in position.

AS-13

Each windowsill is made from 2×6 pressure-treated lumber cut to 42" long. Rip the front and back edge at an angle of 15 degrees, as the sill will be installed at this angle for drainage. From the back of each end, cut a section 4½" wide x 4¼" deep, to leave two narrow wings that will extend beyond the window opening. The back of the sill should be flush with the back of the interior wall frame. Fix the sill in place with long screws through the studs. **(See photo AS-14.)**

The other three sides of the window opening are lined with 1×6, ripped to match the thickness of the walls. Cut and fit the top piece first, to the full width of the opening. Shim as necessary to make sure you have allowed the right clearance for the window at top and bottom. Attach the two side pieces in the same way.

AS-14

Our windows are hinged at the top, with an interior retainer so they can't open too far—side-opening windows that swing freely are a hazard for anyone on the deck outside. We used simple butt hinges, attached to the window and top frame. There's also a 1×2 draft excluder/drip strip around the window opening.

The outside of the window is finished with 1×4 trim. As a little extra flourish, the top trim has angled ends that extend beyond the sides. The trim is repeated on the inside. **(See photo AS-15.)**

The 6'×30" Dutch door is made of two layers. The inside is vertical 1×6 cedar tongue & groove, the outer regular 1×6 cedar. The lower section is 36" tall, the upper 30"—if they were equal, the lower half would look smaller. **(See photo AS-16.)**

First cut the sections of tongue and groove. We planned to edge the finished door with 1×2 all round as another nice little detail, and therefore cut the boards to measure 28½" wide x 34½" high for the lower panel and 28½" × 28½" for the upper. Rip the outer boards equally so that the joins are symmetrical—we're going to make a feature of this door.

On a flat surface, set out the pieces of tongue & groove for the lower panel with the V-groove uppermost. Cut two pieces of 1×6 to 28½" for the top and bottom. Glue and clamp them flush with the edges of the panel, and reinforce with finishing nails. The two side pieces will be about 23½", depending on the exact dimensions of your 1×6. Cut to fit, and attach.

Lay a 1×6 diagonally across the middle of the panel and mark the ends to fit inside the frame. The second diagonal will be a mirror image of this, with a piece cut out at the crossover.

AS-15

AS-16

Cover the edges with strips of 1×2 glued and nailed in place. The corners can be either mitered or square.

The upper panel can be made the same way but we gave it a small window, just because. The Plexiglas panel is 9" square. The frame is made from 6' of leftover hardwood 2×3; both edges of one side are rabbeted to half depth, to fit over the window and the door panel. The corners can be mitered, half-lapped or shoulder-jointed. The icing on the cake is the ½" muntin bars, cross-lapped in the middle and glued into shallow notches in the frame. The Plexiglas is held in place with silicone and a narrow wooden molding.

Use a jigsaw to cut a hole in the door panel. Glue and screw the window in place. On the inside, make a mitered frame out of 1×2 to cover the edges of the hole, and attach with finishing nails.

Cut a 30" length of 2×3 and bevel one edge at 45 degrees. Attach it to the lower edge of the panel so that it will overlap the bottom door. A simple wooden turn-button on the inside will keep both doors together when required.

The top and sides of the doorway are lined with 1×6, ripped to match the thickness of the walls and shimmed as necessary. Use a beveled 2×4 for the threshold.

Trim the front sides of the doorway with 1×4. We made a more ornate lintel out of 2×6, cut to a gentle taper at the ends—it gives the doorway a visual lift.

The door is hung with strap hinges and held shut with a traditional-style clasp. A narrow draft excluder strip completes the doorway.

The corners of the treehouse are finished with a vertical trim of 1×3 and 1×4 cedar. Attach the 1×3 to the sidewalls, and overlap it with 1×4 at front and back. A bevel-cut 1×4 finishes the base of the walls all round.

Cut a piece of 1×6 cedar for the eaves, to finish flush with the outside of the front and rear 2×4 joists. Attach to the tails of all the joists.

Cut and fit 1×6 cedar facings to the 2×4 at the gables. It's worth taking to time make a really neat join here.

TREEHOUSE LOCKS & LATCHES

Of course you can always buy plain or fancy latches for your treehouse, but you might like to make the place even more special with a handmade wooden lock. Here's a couple of ideas, and you can use the same principles to design something unique—the possibilities are endless.

Hidden Lock

Pulling an inconspicuous rope from the outside can open the door.

Note: View shown here is from the inside of the house. **(See Fig. 1.)**

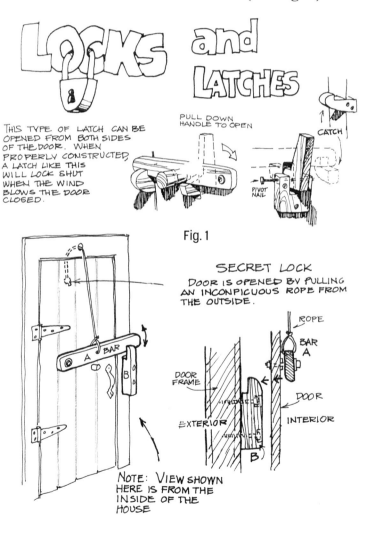

THIS TYPE OF LATCH CAN BE OPENED FROM BOTH SIDES OF THE DOOR. WHEN PROPERLY CONSTRUCTED, A LATCH LIKE THIS WILL LOCK SHUT WHEN THE WIND BLOWS THE DOOR CLOSED.

PULL DOWN HANDLE TO OPEN

CATCH

PIVOT NAIL

Fig. 1

SECRET LOCK
DOOR IS OPENED BY PULLING AN INCONPICUOUS ROPE FROM THE OUTSIDE.

A BAR

B

ROPE

BAR A

DOOR FRAME

DOOR

EXTERIOR

INTERIOR

B

NOTE: VIEW SHOWN HERE IS FROM THE INSIDE OF THE HOUSE

ROPE WORK

A rope railing on your treehouse deck can give it an airy feeling and allows you to feel more a part of nature. If you are using rope on your treehouse railing, these illustrations should help you cut, whip, and seal it.

For ropes, check out R & W Rope Warehouse, 866-577-5505.

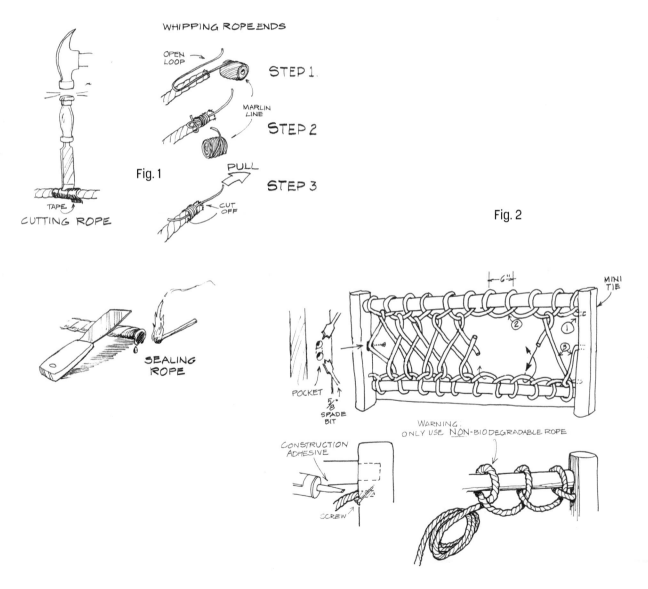

WHIPPING ROPE ENDS

OPEN LOOP

STEP 1

MARLIN LINE

STEP 2

Fig. 1

PULL

STEP 3

CUT OFF

TAPE
CUTTING ROPE

Fig. 2

SEALING ROPE

MINI TIE

6"

POCKET
5/8" SPADE BIT

WARNING.
ONLY USE NON-BIODEGRADABLE ROPE

CONSTRUCTION ADHESIVE

SCREW

TRANSPORT WAGON

The treehouse builder's secret weapon: an all-terrain vehicle! We often have to carry tools from the driveway to the treehouse building site, which can be quite a distance. We use this wagon for carrying the lumber and tools and find it very helpful. It is quick and easy to build. All it requires is a sheet of plywood, a 2×4, four heavy-duty caster type wheels, and some rope. It can also be used for other purposes—from hauling firewood to moving heavy equipment. The wide tires are specifically chosen to help prevent leaving deep ruts in the lawn. We asked our client's kids to help us pull the wagon and they gladly chipped in to everyone's enjoyment!

MATERIALS

Qty.	Size	Description	Location
(1)	3'×4'	¾" AC plywood	Bottom
(2)	4' long	2×4 const. fir	Sides
(1)	10' long	⅝" thick rope	Pull
(2)	10"	Heavy-duty rigid pneumatic	Rear caster wheels
(2)	10"	Heavy-duty swivel	Front caster wheels

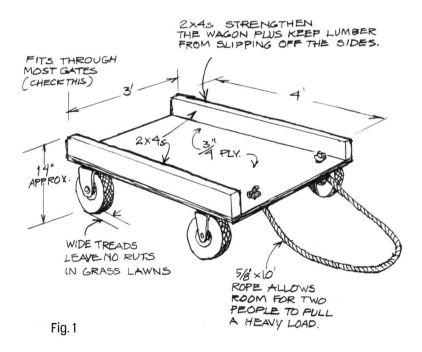

2X4s STRENGTHEN THE WAGON PLUS KEEP LUMBER FROM SLIPPING OFF THE SIDES.

FITS THROUGH MOST GATES (CHECK THIS)

3'

4'

2X4s

¾" PLY.

14" APPROX.

WIDE TREADS LEAVE NO RUTS IN GRASS LAWNS

⅝"×10' ROPE ALLOWS ROOM FOR TWO PEOPLE TO PULL A HEAVY LOAD.

Fig. 1

AERIAL OBSTACLES

What could be better than a treehouse? Well, maybe two treehouses—or more! At the time of writing we are working on a group of three—one fully enclosed, with surrounding deck, and two smaller open platforms. They will be connected by three bridges of different types: a solid boardwalk leading from the treehouse deck, a gently swaying plank bridge on cables, and—the most adventurous—a single thick rope, with rope handrail and safety netting on either side. We're also including a mixture of wooden ladders, staircases, rope ladders, and climbing nets to provide different routes up or down; the solid bridge has monkey bars built in underneath. This offers endless possibilities for play, relaxation, and sport.

Any connection between treehouses has to allow for tree growth and movement; this is relatively easy with the inherent stretch of a rope or cable bridge, but a solid structure should be flexibly attached—for example, by making it overlong so that it rests on top of the deck at one end. Ropes and their supports must be securely anchored, and don't skimp on hardware: the eyebolts and shackles sold in hardware stores are unlikely to be rated for play structures or off-ground use. In the United States we've used:

www.e-rigging.com
www.ropes.courses
www.ExperientialSystems.com

Part Three
Nature Playgrounds

This section features play structures made mostly from logs—leave the bark on to let them blend in with the natural environment, or strip off the bark and sand the wood smooth. Many of the logs will be set in the ground, so it's important that the wood be rot-resistant or treated with preservative. Rot-resistant species include locust, red mulberry, Osage orange, and yew. Tropical woods such as ipe, lignum vitae, purple heart, and old-growth teak are also durable. Consider also cedar, cypress, redwood, and white oak, which can last well if treated. Another good option is pressure-treated wood (generally southern pine) that can last up to 40 years in the ground.

If you want something to last for your grandchildren, you might want to look for peeled black-locust logs. It is sometimes claimed to last 60 years. Many public "nature playgrounds" are using this wood today. (See: Robidecking.com.) Unfortunately, black locust is sometimes difficult to obtain, as it's not grown commercially, although it lines many of the streets in New York City. It can be identified by the dark, rough bark, and occasionally by large sharp thorns growing from the trunk. In the fall, the trees shed conspicuous seedpods 3" or 4" long.

Aromatic red cedar can last almost as long in the ground as pressure-treated posts. To make it even more decay-resistant, put preservative or black roofing tar on the portion of the log that will be in the ground. Make sure to protect the log from backsplash and melting snow by extending the preservative at least ten inches above ground. You can apply liquid preservative by wrapping the bottom of the post in plastic and pouring the preservative inside to let it soak in overnight. Watch out for sprinkler systems that can soak the posts on a nightly basis—this can really accelerate rot. Wrapping the bottom of posts with copper shields is a good way to protect the posts from damage by Weedwackers.

If you don't have any trees you want to take down in your yard, check with tree services and see if they have any suitable small trees that were destined for the chipper. You might also try

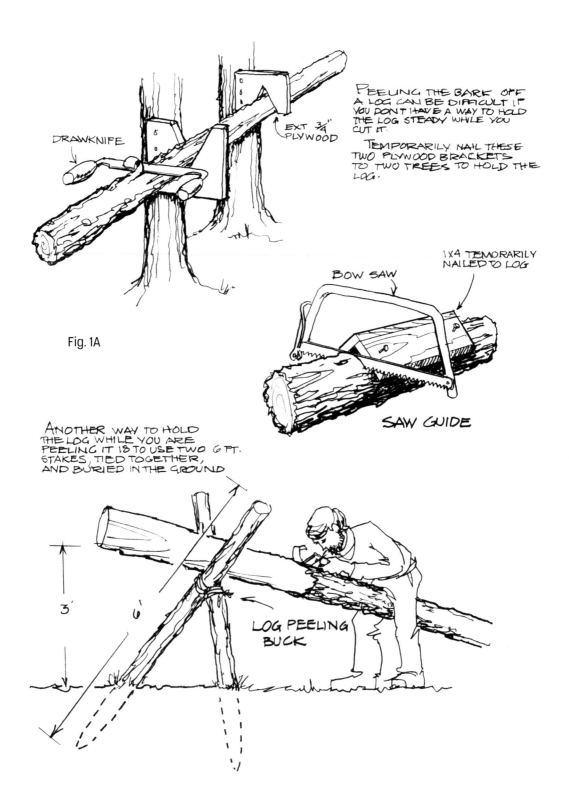

DRAWKNIFE

EXT 3/4" PLYWOOD

PEELING THE BARK OFF A LOG CAN BE DIFFICULT IF YOU DON'T HAVE A WAY TO HOLD THE LOG STEADY WHILE YOU CUT IT.

TEMPORARILY NAIL THESE TWO PLYWOOD BRACKETS TO TWO TREES TO HOLD THE LOG.

Fig. 1A

BOW SAW

1X4 TEMORARILY NAILED TO LOG

SAW GUIDE

ANOTHER WAY TO HOLD THE LOG WHILE YOU ARE PEELING IT IS TO USE TWO 6 FT. STAKES, TIED TOGETHER, AND BURIED IN THE GROUND

3'

6'

LOG PEELING BUCK

Fig. 1B

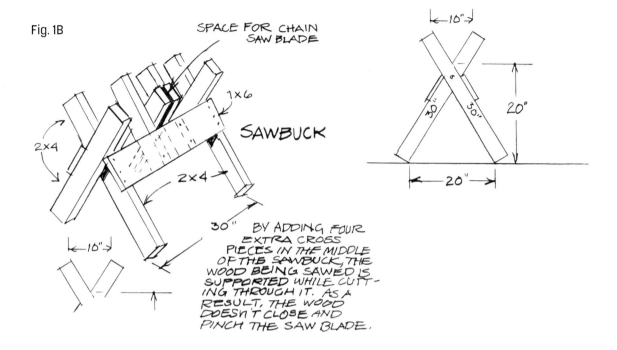

SPACE FOR CHAIN SAW BLADE

1×6

SAWBUCK

2×4

2×4

30"

2×4

10"

10"

20"

30"

30"

20"

BY ADDING FOUR EXTRA CROSS PIECES IN THE MIDDLE OF THE SAWBUCK, THE WOOD BEING SAWED IS SUPPORTED WHILE CUTTING THROUGH IT. AS A RESULT, THE WOOD DOESN'T CLOSE AND PINCH THE SAW BLADE.

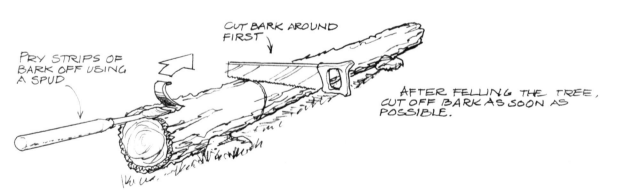

CUT BARK AROUND FIRST

PRY STRIPS OF BARK OFF USING A SPUD

AFTER FELLING THE TREE, CUT OFF BARK AS SOON AS POSSIBLE.

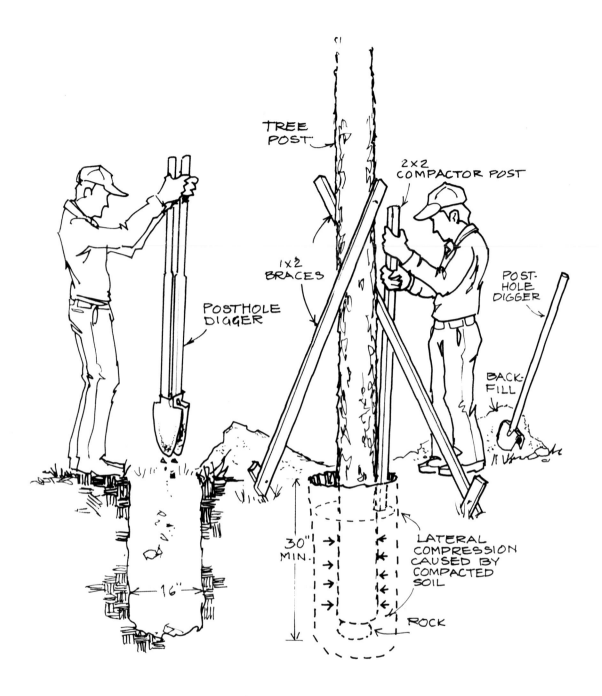

TREE POST

2×2 COMPACTOR POST

1×2 BRACES

POSTHOLE DIGGER

POSTHOLE DIGGER

BACK-FILL

30" MIN.

16"

LATERAL COMPRESSION CAUSED BY COMPACTED SOIL

ROCK

Fig. 2

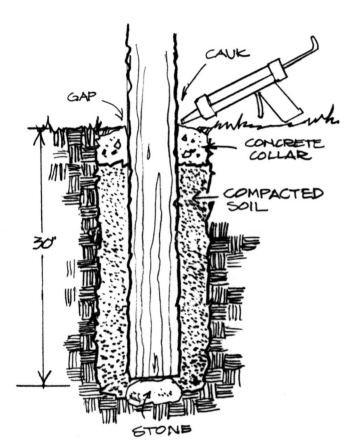

GAP

CAUK

CONCRETE
COLLAR

COMPACTED
SOIL

30"

STONE

AFTER A FEW YEARS A GAP MAY
APPEAR ALLOWING WATER TO
PENETRATE AND ROT THE POST.

FILL THE GAP WITH SILICONE
CAULK.

Fig. 3

firewood sellers, fencing suppliers, and landscape and garden stores. Peeled logs, especially pressure-treated logs used in vineyards, tend to last longer than logs with the bark on; keep this in mind when you decide how long you want your play structure to last. **(See. Fig. 1A and Fig. 1B.)**

Peeling Red Cedar

The stringy shaggy bark of red cedar can be peeled off using a power washer. The best time to peel the tree is right after it has been cut down, preferably in the spring, when the sap is running. Once it has dried, sand the stubs of the branches smooth, to leave them aesthetically pleasing and easy to touch.

The center of the wood (heartwood) is purple in color and gives off a nice cedar scent; this core is dense and will retain its strength after the outer portion of the log has decayed. The heartwood is valued for its aromatic cedar scent, and chips are sold to keep moths out of closets.

Installing Posts

If possible, you should try to bury wood posts below the frost line in your area, to keep them from heaving. Dig a hole using a shovel or a hand posthole digger. If the soil is rocky or hard clay, you may need an iron bar to loosen it. You can also hire an excavator to drill out the holes with an auger, assuming there is room for the machine to access your backyard.

Placing the Post

Some builders like to place a flat stone in the bottom of the hole under the post to spread the load. Most tree posts under 15' can be lifted into place by two or three people. Stand a wide plank in the hole to guide the butt of the post into place as you lift; station your tallest volunteer furthest from the hole, with the shortest person closest. Use an 8' 2×4 to pry up the top end, and place logs under the post as you move forward; when the log end is waist high, give a lift and push all together, dropping the post into the hole. If there is a tree nearby that you can use as a stationary point to lift the log with a block and tackle, all the better.

Backfilling

When backfilling, use a 2×4 to tamp down the soil firmly as you fill the hole. If the exact location of the post is critical, you can brace it temporarily in place with 1×2 supports and make any adjustments before backfilling—for example, when making a rectangular structure to specific dimensions.

For an extra-solid installation, we often fill the hole with quick-set concrete, which doesn't need premixing; follow the instructions on the bag. It generally takes two 80-lb. bags per hole. Slope the top of the concrete to help water drain off. **(See Fig. 2 and Fig. 3.)**

NATURE HUT

If you are lucky enough to live where there are trees surrounding your house, you might like to build this hut to claim your own space in the backyard, take a break from the adventure course and chill out! All you need is a small pruning saw to cut the branches and some rope.

Find two saplings that are growing close to each other, around 6' apart. Bend the tops over and tie them together with thin rope. **(See Fig. 1.)**

Add a ridgepole to the back and tie it to the two saplings.

Add more saplings or long, straight branches to the structure. Once that is done, tie horizontal sticks to the saplings to create a frame.

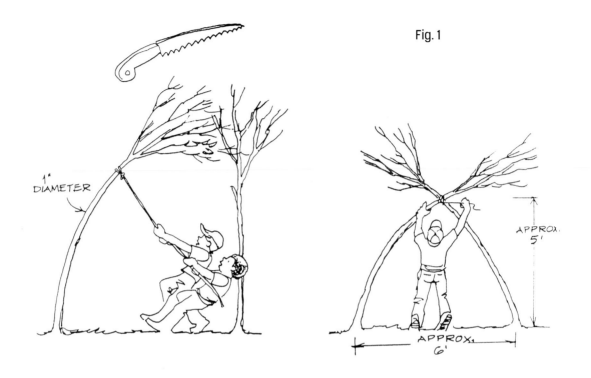

Fig. 1

Cover the frame with pine boughs, twigs, and leaves to create a camouflaged secret hut. **(See Fig. 2.)**

RIDGEPOLE

Fig. 2

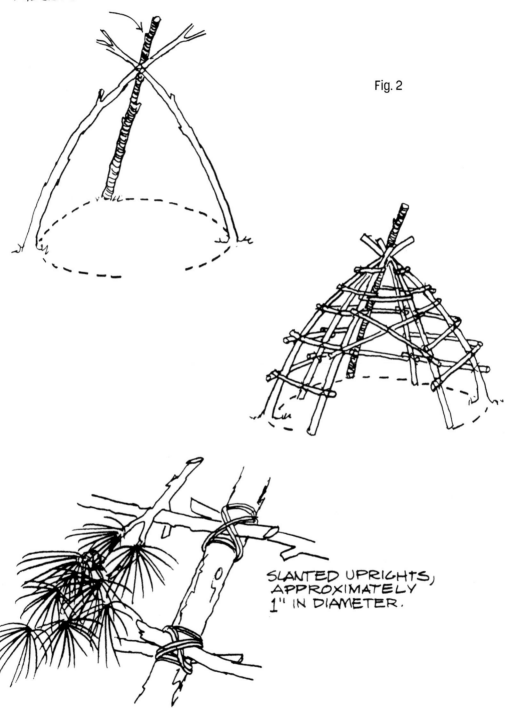

SLANTED UPRIGHTS,
APPROXIMATELY
1" IN DIAMETER.

BALANCE BEAM

If you need a tree cut down on your property, don't just feed it into a chipper! Here is a great way to make your kids happy and give the tree a new life. You will need a straight length of the trunk (we used a section 9' long) and some basic tools as used by our predecessors, like an axe and wedges. (If you don't have a tree, you can adapt this idea using a regular log or pressure-treated post.)

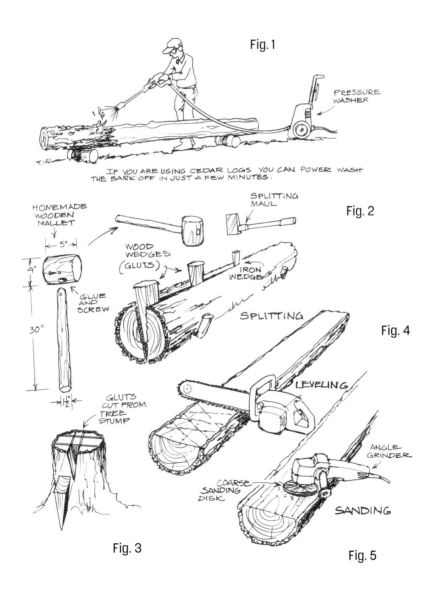

Fig. 1

PRESSURE WASHER

IF YOU ARE USING CEDAR LOGS YOU CAN POWER WASH THE BARK OFF IN JUST A FEW MINUTES.

HOMEMADE WOODEN MALLET

SPLITTING MAUL

Fig. 2

WOOD WEDGES (GLUTS)

IRON WEDGE

SPLITTING

5"

4"

GLUE AND SCREW

30"

Fig. 4

LEVELING

1½"

GLUTS CUT FROM TREE STUMP

ANGLE GRINDER

COARSE SANDING DISK

SANDING

Fig. 3

Fig. 5

The challenge of the balance beam is to run up one side toward the middle, wait for the beam to swing down on the other side, and then run down while keeping your balance. It can also be used as a teeter-totter or seesaw. You can leave the log in the round or split it to flatten the top.

Tip: If you are using cedar logs, try using a power washer to remove the bark. **(See Fig. 1.)**

Use an axe to cut off the branch stubs flush with the surface of the log. If you are going to flatten the top, snap a chalk line down the length of the log, dividing it in half. Next, hammer an iron wedge into one end of the log to create a crack. To keep the crack open while you hammer in another wedge, pound a wooden wedge (called a "glut") into the crack. You can make your own gluts out of the remaining stump or any piece of wood. **(See Fig. 3.)** Following the chalk line, continue pounding wedges in until you feel the log beginning to split and cut away any remaining portions with an axe until the log splits in two. **(See Fig. 2 and Fig. 3.)**

Choose the piece that looks the best. If you are competent using a chainsaw, begin leveling the top surface. Hold the chainsaw so that it is just barely touching the wood surface and move the cutter bar back and forth in a crisscross fashion, being careful not to let the teeth of the saw cut into the wood. **(See Fig. 4.)** It doesn't have to be perfectly flat—in fact, it might be more interesting if it has some wobbles on it. It should, however be splinter-free, and this can be achieved by using an angle grinder with coarse-grit sandpaper, followed by medium, then fine grit. **(See Fig. 5.)**

The balance beam is mounted on two posts. They can be made from parts of the tree or 6×6 pressure-treated posts. You will need two pieces, 45" long. Bury them about 30" in the ground, leaving space for the log beam to fit in-between. Drill a 2"-diameter hole through both posts, about 10" up from the ground. **(See Fig. 6.)**

You will need a length of 1½" galvanized pipe, a length of 2" galvanized pipe, two 2" pipe bracket supports, two 1½" pipe caps, and four ⅜"×4" lag screws bought from your local plumbing store.

Cut out a flat surface on the underside of the midpoint of the beam to accept the pipe brackets and put the axle together. **(See Fig. 7.)**

For brackets, check out mcmastercarr.com.

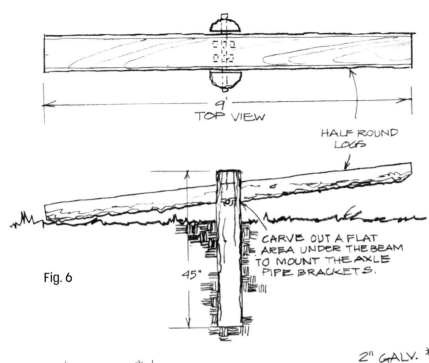

TOP VIEW

9'

HALF ROUND LOGS

Fig. 6

45"

CARVE OUT A FLAT AREA UNDER THE BEAM TO MOUNT THE AXLE PIPE BRACKETS.

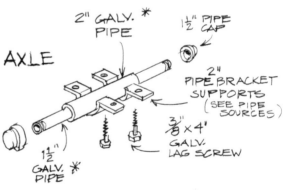

AXLE

2" GALV. PIPE ✱

1½" PIPE CAP

2" PIPE BRACKET SUPPORTS (SEE PIPE SOURCES)

1½" GALV. PIPE ✱

⅜" X 4" GALV. LAG SCREW

Fig. 7

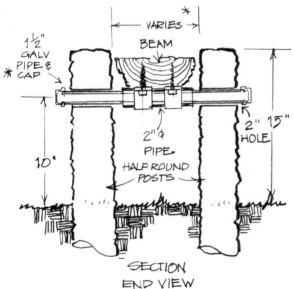

VARIES ✱

BEAM

1½" GALV PIPE & ✱ CAP

2" 15" HOLE

2"∅ PIPE

10"

HALF ROUND POSTS

SECTION END VIEW

✱ NOTE
LENGTH OF PIPE VARIES ACCORDING TO WIDTH OF BEAM.

CLIMBING BARS

This set of climbing bars has strong visual appeal and is always an instant favorite; there can be lots of different ways to reach the top and kids will have a great time discovering them all, perhaps making up their own rules in the process. It's based on a group of sturdy posts approximately 6–10" in diameter. We recommend using eight or ten of them—or more—to make it interesting and challenging. Use posts of various lengths; around 5–15' is a good range, and allows for 30–36" to be buried in the ground.

Begin by scribing a rough circle on the ground and removing any obstacles such as stumps, rocks, or roots.

Plant the largest post securely in the center of the area, using concrete if necessary. Measure out from the post approximately 18" inches, plus the radius of the second post, and mark the center with a stake. Mark the remaining posts in the same way and readjust the stakes until you're happy with the layout, making sure the gaps between posts are around 18" so the children can easily get through. **(See Fig. 1.)**

Fig. 1

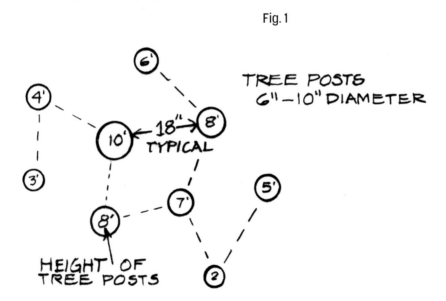

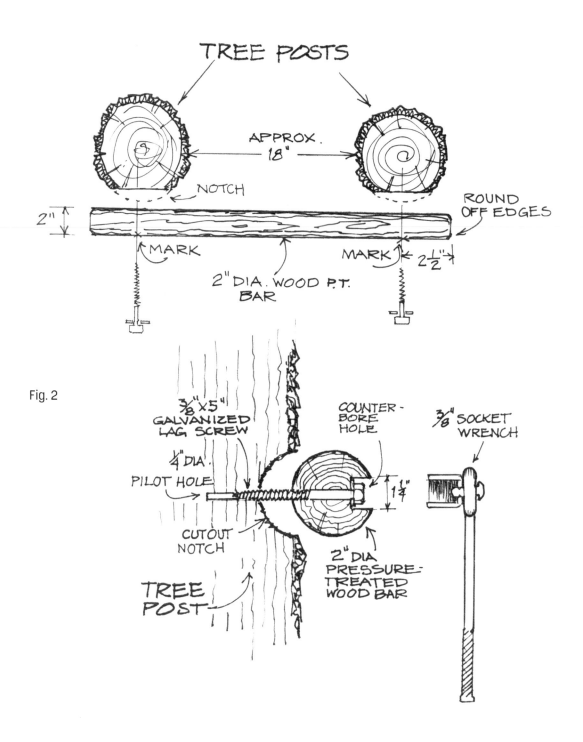

TREE POSTS

APPROX. 18"

NOTCH

ROUND OFF EDGES

2"

MARK

MARK

2½"

2" DIA. WOOD P.T. BAR

Fig. 2

⅜" X 5" GALVANIZED LAG SCREW

¼" DIA. PILOT HOLE

COUNTER-BORE HOLE

⅜" SOCKET WRENCH

1¼"

CUTOUT NOTCH

2" DIA PRESSURE-TREATED WOOD BAR

TREE POST

Dig out all the holes and loosely place the posts to make sure the arrangement looks right. Think about how the kids will move from one to the next, as they move up, down, and across. Backfill and/or concrete the posts in place. Dig out the area around the posts to a depth of 12" and fill with soft bark chips.

The 2"-diameter climbing bars can be made from a naturally rot-resistant wood such as black locust or from pressure-treated posts. When deciding where to place the bars, imagine you are a child trying to climb the structure, and try to provide several different ways to reach the top. It should be challenging but not impossible—make sure each bar is accessible for the intended age group.

The bars must be sanded smooth, and the ends carefully rounded. To join a bar to the tree posts, temporarily place it across two posts at the desired height and mark 2½" from each end of the bar. Drill a ½"-deep, 1¼"-diameter counter-bore hole to provide clearance for the lag-screw head. Drill a ⅜" hole through the bar. Holding the bar in place, drill a ¼" pilot hole into the post. To make the joint stronger and more attractive, carve out a curved notch in the post with chisel and rasp. Secure the bar to the posts with ⅜"×5" galvanized lag screws and washers, using a ⅜" socket wrench. **(See Fig. 2.)**

Tip: Attach a bell at the top of the tallest post, so the kids can announce to everybody within hearing distance that they made it!

SAFETY
BUFFER

SAFETY
BUFFER

RUSTIC SWING

This classic traditional swing never ceases to please small kids and big-kid adults alike. It lets you "fly through the air with the greatest of ease" without a care in the world—but wait a minute, not so fast. Keep an eye on those flying feet up in the air, and don't build another project too close to the swing. **(See Fig. 1.)**

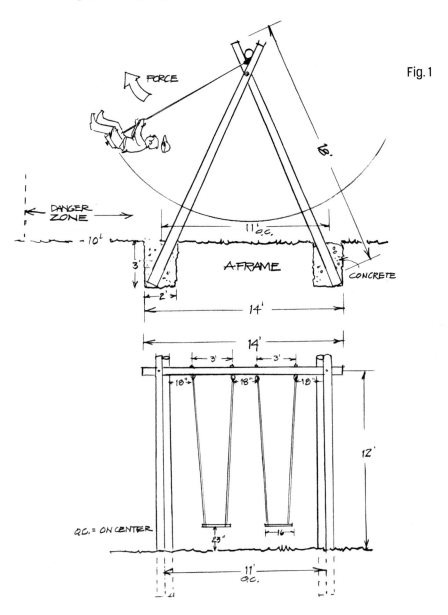

Fig. 1

Fig. 2

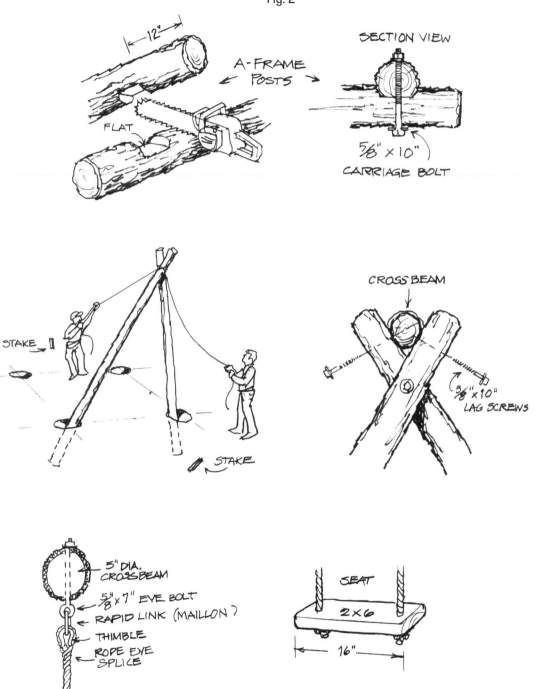

12"

A-FRAME
POSTS

FLAT

SECTION VIEW

5/8" X 10"
CARRIAGE BOLT

STAKE

STAKE

CROSS BEAM

5/8" X 10"
LAG SCREWS

5" DIA.
CROSSBEAM

5/8" X 7" EYE BOLT

RAPID LINK (MAILLON?)

THIMBLE

ROPE EYE
SPLICE

SEAT

2 X 6

16"

The log swing requires four straight poles (trees) 18' long and one 14' long—with or without bark—approximately 5" in diameter. Be sure to inspect the wood to see that it's structurally sound throughout. To have a really good look, remove any bark with a power washer or draw-knife.

Lay the first two poles on the ground and overlap them at the top by 12", with the lower ends about 12' apart. Scribe where they overlap, and cut a notch in both poles to match, using a chainsaw.

Squeeze some construction adhesive on the joint, and bolt the poles together using a ⅝" x 10" galvanized or stainless-steel carriage bolt with a nut and washer. Do the same with the other pair of poles, and allow them to set overnight. Dig four 3'-deep holes.

In preparation for the lift, plant two stakes in the ground 8'–10' from where the A-frame will be set and attach ropes to the top of the A-frame to help lift and steady the frame. You can tie off the ropes to the stakes once the frame is in place.

Once the poles are in place and the concrete is ready, call the folks at home to come out with their cameras to watch (and help!) you—you'll want a couple of them to hold the ropes. After the poles are upright in the ground, fill each hole with four 80-lb. bags of quick-set concrete. Using plenty of concrete will help to anchor the frame in the ground.

When the concrete has set (overnight), two people on 10' ladders can lift the crossbeam onto the "V" notches formed by the posts. To secure the beam, drill a ½" pilot hole through each post and partly into the crossbeam, and firmly attach a ⅝"×10" long lag screw with washer.

Install the ⅝" ropes for the swings by drilling two ¾"-diameter holes, 36" apart, vertically through the crossbeam for the two swings. (You can also do this earlier while the beam is on the ground—if so, make sure the holes are still vertical before securing the beam to the support posts.)

Insert a ⅝" x 7" stainless-steel eyebolt into each hole and secure it with a washer, lock washer, and nut. Buy four ropes 12' long with an eye splice and thimble on the end. (See marine catalogs for dock lines.) Connect the ropes to the eyebolts with stainless-steel rapid links (maillons). Use only hardware specifically rated for play equipment, such as that sold by rope. courses or e-rigging.com (USA).

Make the two seats out of 2×6 hardwood, cut 16" long, rounded & sanded smooth. Drill a ¾" hole in each end and thread the rope through with a stop knot. **(See Fig. 2.)**

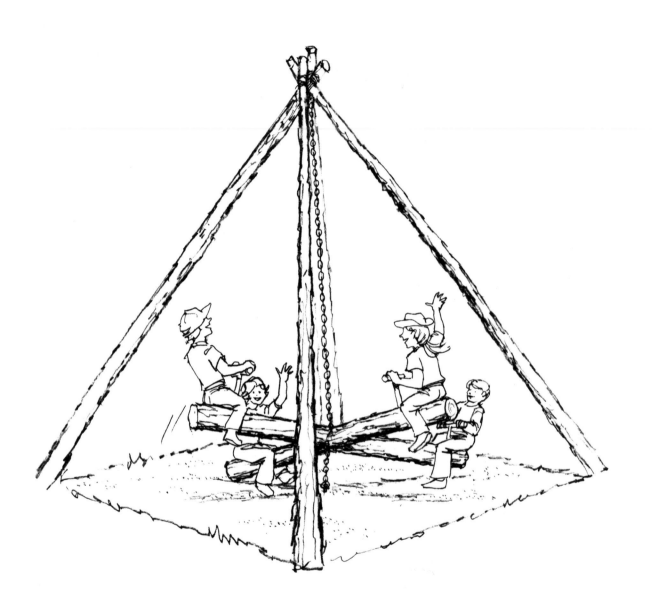

BUCKING BRONCO

This triple-action swing is somewhat like riding a bucking bronco, as it moves in several directions at once. It moves up and down like a seesaw, spins around in a circle—and tilts when there are four riders.

To build the bucking bronco you will need four straight logs for the stand, measuring approximately 5" at the base to 4" at the top and about 18' long. You will also need two 8–10"-diameter logs 10' long, for the kids to sit on. **(See Fig. 1.)**

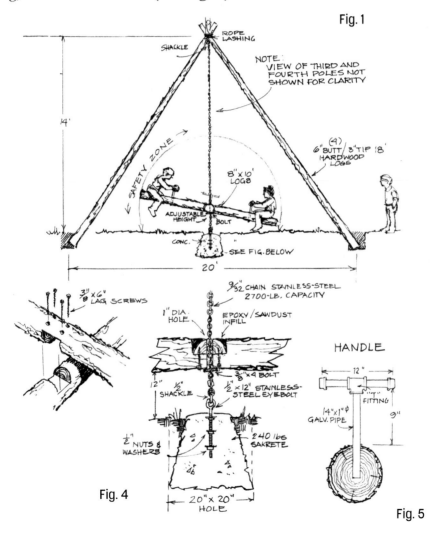

Fig. 1

Fig. 2

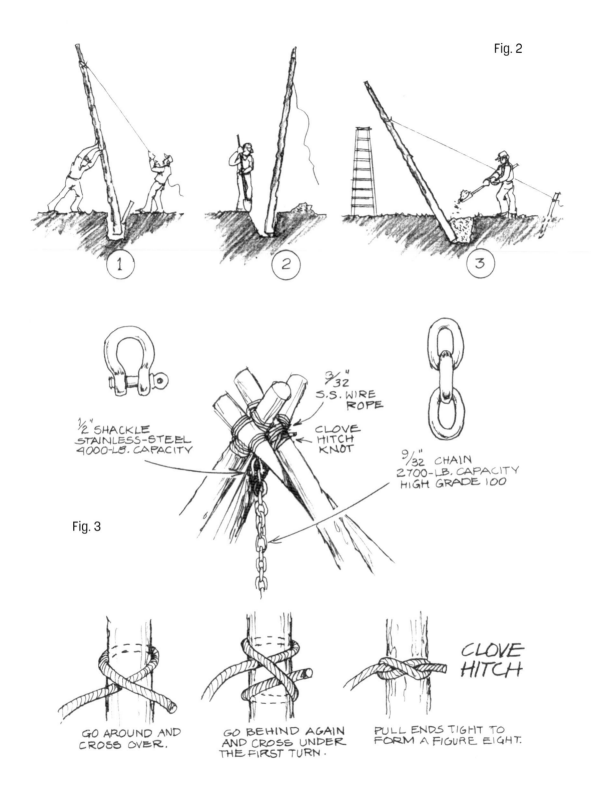

① ② ③

½" SHACKLE
STAINLESS-STEEL
4000-LB. CAPACITY

3/32" S.S. WIRE ROPE

CLOVE HITCH KNOT

9/32" CHAIN
2700-LB. CAPACITY
HIGH GRADE 100

Fig. 3

GO AROUND AND
CROSS OVER.

GO BEHIND AGAIN
AND CROSS UNDER
THE FIRST TURN.

PULL ENDS TIGHT TO
FORM A FIGURE EIGHT.

CLOVE HITCH

Remove the bark and sand all the logs smooth (but not too slippery). Notch out the center of the two cross-logs so that they will nest together when placed across each other. Put them together and secure the joint with four ⅜"×6" lag screws and construction adhesive. Since there will be a lot of pressure on the joint, fill any gaps with a mixture of epoxy resin and sawdust and allow it to cure overnight. Drill a vertical 1"-diameter hole through the middle of the log joint, using a long 1" spade drill.

Dig four 2'-deep holes to form a square 18' apart. Move each pole over one of the holes and place a short 8"-wide board in the hole to allow the pole to slide in easily. Tie a long rope to the top end of the pole and, with the help of a friend, slide the pole into the hole. **(See Fig. 2.)**

Once you have all four poles standing loosely in the holes, dig out the side of the hole that is closest to the center of the square so the pole can lean in. Hold the post in position by securing it with a rope tied to a temporary stake in the ground. Follow the same procedure with the other three poles and lash them together at the top with ⅜" nylon rope. **(See Fig. 3.)** Finish the top by lashing a ½" stainless-steel shackle to all four poles using 3⁄32" stainless-steel cable. Dig a 20x20" hole in the ground in the middle of the four poles and attach a 15' length of 9⁄32" stainless-steel chain to the shackle. Fill the hole in the ground with three 80lb. bags of concrete; while the concrete is still wet, insert a ½" x 12" long stainless-steel eyebolt with four nuts and washers attached to it. This gives the concrete more gripping power. **(See Fig. 4.)**

Prop the crossbeams up approximately 12" from the ground, and insert a ⅜" x 4" stainless-steel bolt with nuts and washers through a link in the chain to support the beams. The height of the beams can be adjusted as the kids grow taller. Attach the bottom of the chain to the eyebolt using another ½" stainless-steel shackle.

The kids will need something to hold on to, just like the rodeo riders do. For each handle, use 14" of 1" pipe (threaded at both ends), a 1" tee-fitting; four 4" nipples, and four end caps. These are available from plumbing stores. Fit the pieces together. **(See Fig. 5.)**

Drill a 1" hole into each end of the beams, and insert the assembled handles.

RUSTIC LOG SEATING

Making seats and benches out of logs and branches is a great way to use up leftover wood.

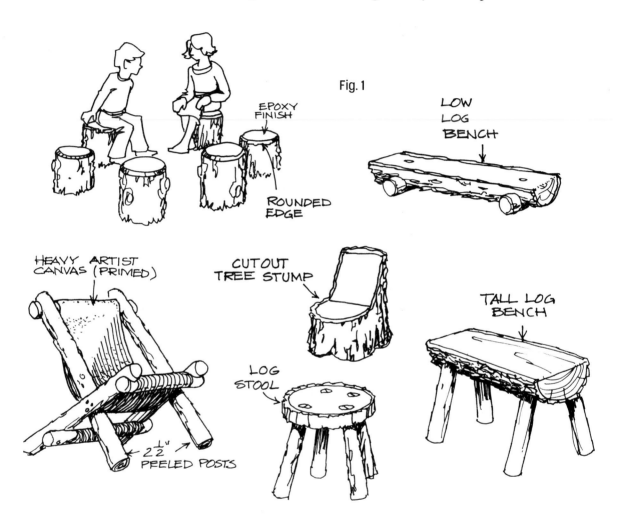

Fig. 1

EPOXY FINISH

ROUNDED EDGE

LOW LOG BENCH

HEAVY ARTIST CANVAS (PRIMED)

CUTOUT TREE STUMP

TALL LOG BENCH

LOG STOOL

$2\frac{1}{2}$" PEELED POSTS

Part Four
Timeless DIY Projects & Games

The projects in this section are simple, classic designs that have been enjoyed by—and often made by—kids for a long time. As we've shown throughout this book, fun doesn't have to be electronic. It doesn't have to be complicated or expensive to make either, and the whole family can join in.

LEMONADE STAND

This lemonade stand is simply a box made from scrap lumber, attached to an old bicycle wheel. The dimensions we used are based on a 12"-diameter wheel. If your wheel is a different size, you can adjust the height of the front bracket support (see sketch) to make the box level. **(See Fig. 1.)**

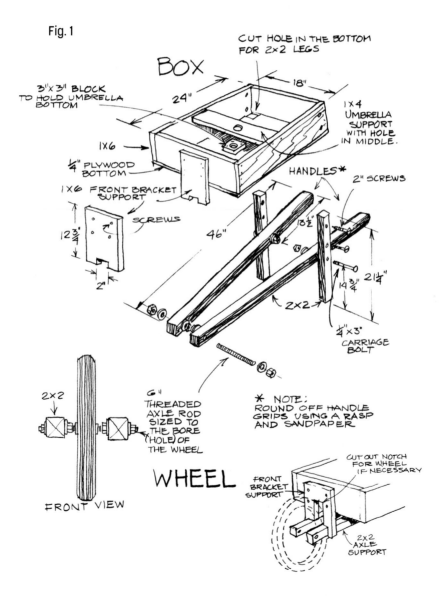

Fig. 1

BOX

CUT HOLE IN THE BOTTOM
FOR 2X2 LEGS

3"X3" BLOCK
TO HOLD UMBRELLA
BOTTOM

24"

18"

1X4
UMBRELLA
SUPPORT
WITH HOLE
IN MIDDLE.

1X6

¼" PLYWOOD
BOTTOM

1X6 FRONT BRACKET
SUPPORT

SCREWS

HANDLES*

2" SCREWS

12¾"

46"

13½"

2"

2X2

21¼"

14¾"

¼"X3"
CARRIAGE
BOLT

2X2

6"
THREADED
AXLE ROD
SIZED TO
THE BORE
(HOLE) OF
THE WHEEL

* NOTE:
ROUND OFF HANDLE
GRIPS USING A RASP
AND SANDPAPER

WHEEL

FRONT VIEW

CUT OUT NOTCH
FOR WHEEL
IF NECESSARY

FRONT
BRACKET
SUPPORT

2X2
AXLE
SUPPORT

Getting Started

You will need:

- A large pitcher to pour the lemonade
- A long wooden spoon for mixing
- Lemonade
- Ice cubes in a bucket
- A notebook & pencil or iPad
- A cash box (an old cigar box with slots cut in the top and dividers inside)

Optional: A rain umbrella or beach umbrella and a sign to wave at motorists.

Author's note:

Although instant or premade lemonade is fine, there is nothing better than fresh lemonade made with real lemons, sugar and water. (Charge extra if you use real lemonade!)

Mind Your Own Business

If you are starting your own business selling lemonade, here are a couple useful tips before beginning:

Materials: Check the kitchen for available supplies. If the cupboard is bare, make a list of what you need: lemonade, cookies, paper cups.

Sales and Profit: Keep track of your sales and at the end of the day, subtract your expenses (cups, lemonade mix, maybe cookies). What's left is your profit!

SECRET LOCKBOX

All kids need a box to keep their secret stuff in. This strong lockbox looks impossible to open unless you know the secret. (It opens in the back by pushing in a special spot.)

Make this box by using common 1×6 and 1×3 boards. The back piece swings out by means of two carefully placed pivot nails. Before putting in the nails, groove the bottom piece so that it won't bind when the back closes. **(See Fig. 1.)**

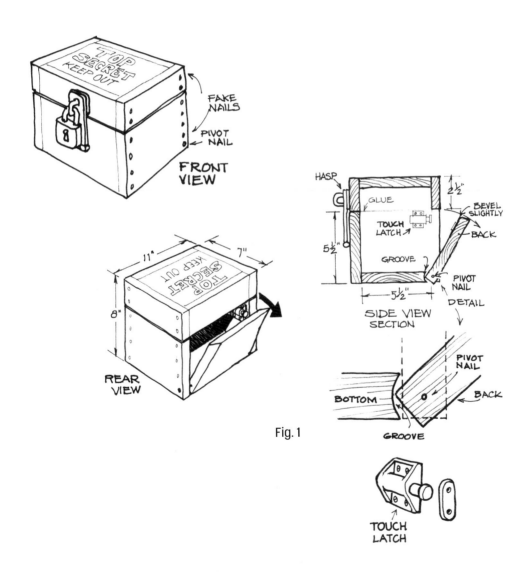

Fig. 1

Treasure Chest...

...WITH A SECRET LOCK

Fig. 1

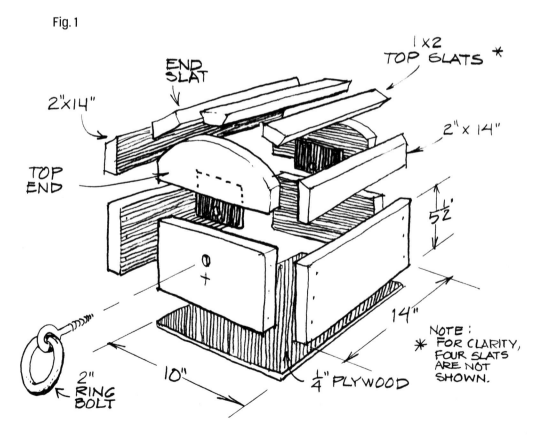

2"X14"

END SLAT

1 X 2 TOP SLATS *

2" X 14"

TOP END

5½"

14"

2" RING BOLT

10"

¼" PLYWOOD

NOTE:
* FOR CLARITY, FOUR SLATS ARE NOT SHOWN.

TREASURE CHEST WITH SECRET LOCK

This treasure chest has a secret lock that only you and your friends will know how to open. It is fairly simple to build: however, you will need an adult to bevel the top pieces using a table saw. The secret to unlocking the treasure chest is in the two steel ring bolts on the sides that have to be turned counterclockwise several times to unlock the top. We found ours at McMaster-Carr Supply Co. www.mcmaster.com.

Making the Chest

Begin by making a 10 × 14" box with a ¼"-thick plywood bottom. Cut the top end pieces, using an electric jigsaw, at a 5½" radius. Bevel the top edges of the 2" x 14" front and back pieces at 20 degrees. Bevel five 1×2 top slats at 7.5 degrees on both edges so that they fit together neatly. Cut two end slats to measure 1¾" wide x 14" long. Bevel one edge of each end slat at 45 degrees to fit the front and back. **(See Fig. 1.)**

Install two trunk catches and a key plate to make it appear that a key is necessary to open the chest.

Glue and nail a 2" x 4" piece of ¼" plywood to the top inside of each side of the chest. Close the chest and drill a hole through the outside of the chest and the inside flap. Screw the ring bolt into the sides and flaps to lock the chest. **(See Fig. 2.)**

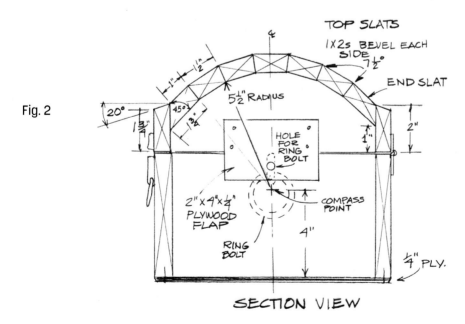

Fig. 2

SECTION VIEW

CIRCLE SWING

This swing should take only a few hours to build. It is made by cutting two 4' circles from a single sheet of ¾" plywood, glued and screwed together. Use ¾" braided rope to secure it to an overhanging tree branch. The seat should be 12–16" off the ground (depending on the size of the kids using it). Drill four equidistant holes, 2" from the edge of the circle. Cut two pieces of rope, approximately 12' long. Thread each rope through two adjacent holes and tie a secure stop knot at each of the four ends. Join the top of the loop to a single rope attached to the tree. To cover the edge of the plywood, use a hose, cut lengthwise and nailed to the edge.

Fig. 1

OLD HOSE

(2) 4'-DIAMETER CIRCLES GLUED TOGETHER

MERRY-GO-ROUND

This backyard merry-go-round is made from a single sheet of ¾" plywood and a cable spool as used by the telephone company to store wire (cable used to run lines from pole to pole). Since the spools can vary in size, it is impossible to give exact dimensions; however the following directions should serve as a useful guide.

If the telephone spool is too tall for your kids to play on, you can bury the bottom half of the spool in the ground. As an extra precaution to keep it from moving, secure it in the ground with six or seven ½" x 10" anchor bolts, set in concrete.

Make the top disk out of two 48"-square pieces of ¾" plywood, cut into a circle and glued and screwed together. Cover the edge of the disks with vinyl marine gunwale (gunnel) edging or an old garden hose, cut lengthwise down the middle.

To draw the circle, make a homemade compass using a thin piece of wood, a nail, and a pencil.

Glue and screw the two pieces of plywood together and cut out the circle using an electric jigsaw. **(See Fig. 1.)**

ENLARGED
DETAIL

GUNWALE
EDGING
(SEE SOURCES)

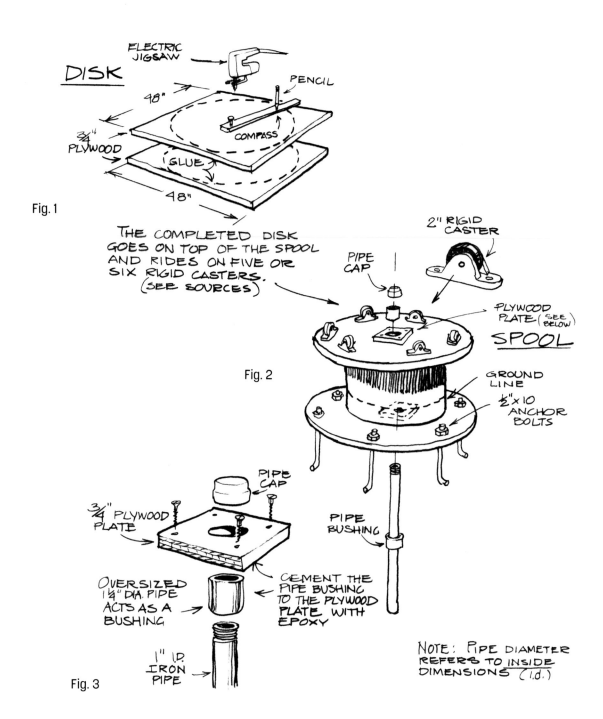

DISK

ELECTRIC JIGSAW

PENCIL

48"

3/4" PLYWOOD

COMPASS

GLUE

48"

Fig. 1

THE COMPLETED DISK GOES ON TOP OF THE SPOOL AND RIDES ON FIVE OR SIX RIGID CASTERS. (SEE SOURCES)

2" RIGID CASTER

PIPE CAP

PLYWOOD PLATE (SEE BELOW)

SPOOL

Fig. 2

GROUND LINE

½"x10 ANCHOR BOLTS

PIPE CAP

3/4" PLYWOOD PLATE

OVERSIZED 1¼" DIA. PIPE ACTS AS A BUSHING

1" I.D. IRON PIPE

PIPE BUSHING

CEMENT THE PIPE BUSHING TO THE PLYWOOD PLATE WITH EPOXY

NOTE: PIPE DIAMETER REFERS TO INSIDE DIMENSIONS (I.D.)

Fig. 3

The completed disk sits on top of the spool and rides on five or six 2" rigid casters (www .northerntool.com) screwed to the top of the spool. **(See Fig. 2.)**

A 1" iron pipe holds the disk in place and is terminated by a pipe cap. Cement the bottom of the pipe into the ground along with the anchor bolts. **(See Fig. 3.)**

If the existing holes in the spool are too large, make them smaller by attaching plywood plates with holes made the same size as the pipe bushings.

Note: Pipe diameter refers to inside dimensions (i.d.).

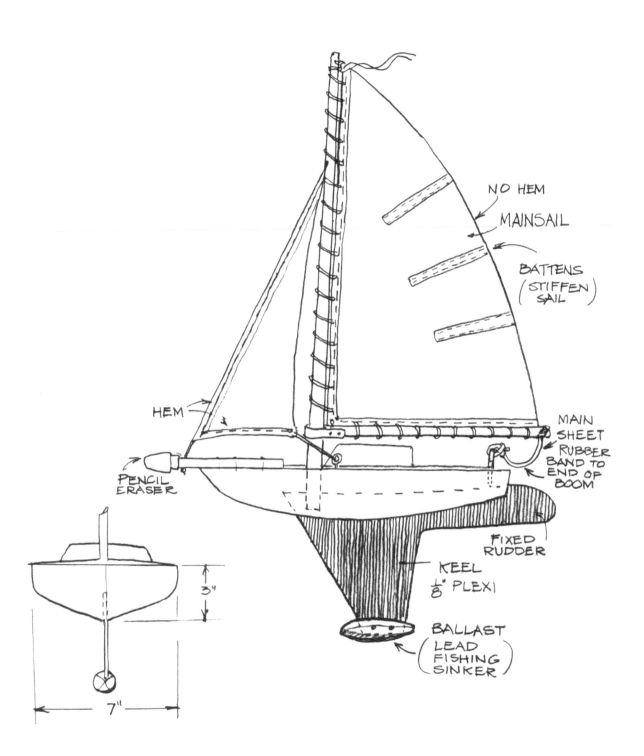

NO HEM

MAINSAIL

BATTENS
(STIFFEN)
SAIL

HEM

MAIN
SHEET
RUBBER
BAND TO
END OF
BOOM

PENCIL
ERASER

FIXED
RUDDER

KEEL
$\frac{1}{8}$" PLEXI

BALLAST
(LEAD
FISHING
SINKER)

3"

7"

MODEL SAILBOAT

What to do on a rainy day? Build a model sailboat for a sunny day! This 19" sailboat may take more than a day to build, but you will have fun building it and even more fun sailing it. Don't worry about the boat sinking: it's made of unsinkable Styrofoam or high-density foam that is easy to carve and shape. It is found at most lumberyards and is used as rigid insulation in house construction. Tip: They often have broken pieces they will give you for free.

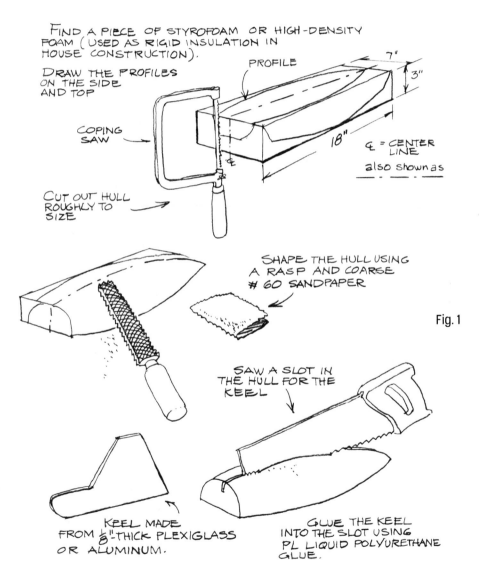

FIND A PIECE OF STYROFOAM OR HIGH-DENSITY FOAM (USED AS RIGID INSULATION IN HOUSE CONSTRUCTION).

DRAW THE PROFILES ON THE SIDE AND TOP

PROFILE

7"

3"

18"

COPING SAW

₡ = CENTER LINE

also shown as

CUT OUT HULL ROUGHLY TO SIZE

SHAPE THE HULL USING A RASP AND COARSE # 60 SANDPAPER

Fig. 1

SAW A SLOT IN THE HULL FOR THE KEEL

KEEL MADE FROM ⅛" THICK PLEXIGLASS OR ALUMINUM.

GLUE THE KEEL INTO THE SLOT USING PL LIQUID POLYURETHANE GLUE.

Fig. 2

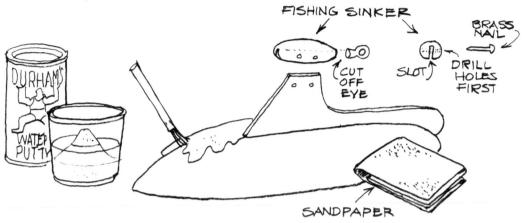

FISHING SINKER

BRASS NAIL

CUT OFF EYE

SLOT

DRILL HOLES FIRST

SANDPAPER

DURHAM'S

WATER PUTTY

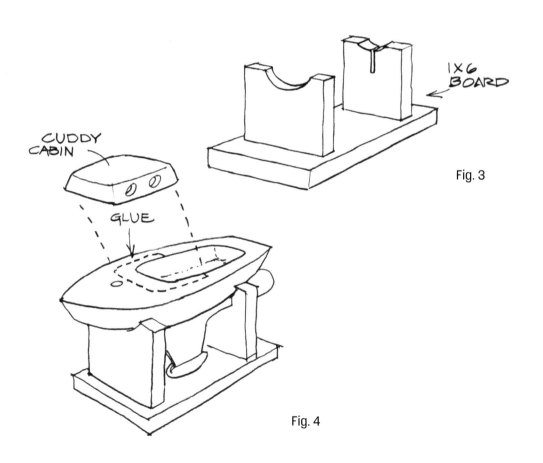

1×6 BOARD

Fig. 3

CUDDY CABIN

GLUE

Fig. 4

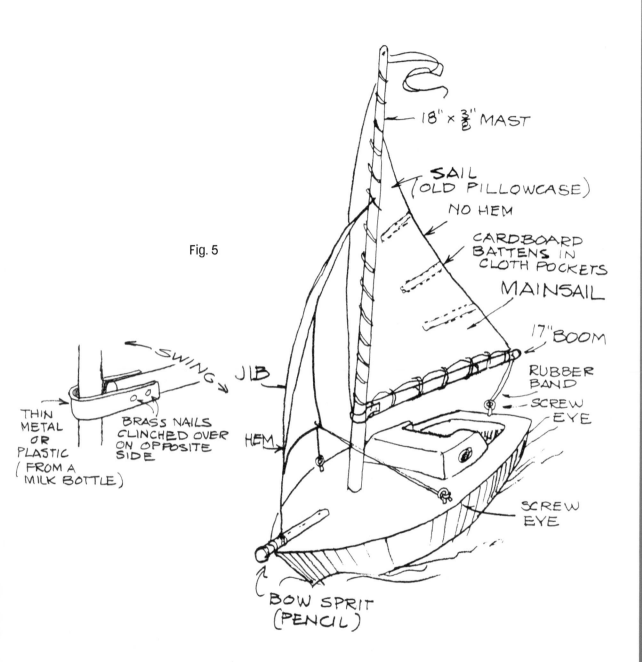

Fig. 5

18" × $\frac{3}{8}$" MAST

SAIL
(OLD PILLOWCASE)

NO HEM

CARDBOARD
BATTENS IN
CLOTH POCKETS

MAINSAIL

17" BOOM

RUBBER
BAND

SCREW
EYE

SCREW
EYE

SWING

JIB

THIN
METAL
OR
PLASTIC
(FROM A
MILK BOTTLE)

BRASS NAILS
CLINCHED OVER
ON OPPOSITE
SIDE

HEM

BOW SPRIT
(PENCIL)

Cover the hull with powdered water putty. Once it has hardened (about 45 minutes), sand it smooth. Using a handsaw, cut a slot in a lead fishing sinker and attach it to the keel with two small brass nails. **(See Fig. 2.)**

It's a good idea to make a stand for the boat. You will need one later on, and it makes it easier to build the rigging, etc. **(See Fig. 3.)**

Carve out the interior to form a cockpit and add a cuddy cabin, also made out of Styrofoam. Cover the topside with water putty, the same as the bottom. **(See Fig. 4.)**

Details

Rig the mast and boom by drilling a ⅜" diameter hole in the deck and inserting a ⅜" x 18" dowel for the mast. Attach the ⅜" x 17" boom to the mast by cutting and bending a piece of metal or plastic to the boom using brass nails.

Cut the sails from an old pillowcase or bedsheet. Hem the forward and bottom edges of the sail, but not the back edges. To stiffen the mainsail, add cardboard battens, sewn into the back of the sail. To hold the boom to the boat, tie a 6" long rubber band to a screw eye on the stern (back) of the boat. Its purpose is to prevent the boat from capsizing under a sudden gust of wind; it will need adjusting to get it right. **(See Fig. 5.)**

POGO BOAT

This is an easy boat to build because it has no curved parts. It will support two people and is great for fishing or just hanging out on the water. It fits easily on top of a car in case you don't live near the water.

You will need:
- (2) 1×12 cedar boards (with no knots), 8' long, for the sides.
- 4×8 sheet of ¼" plywood for the bottom.
- 1×6, 6' long, for the ends.
- 1×10 cedar board for the seats.
- 1×2s 10' long, for the skids and seat supports.
- Waterproof glue, screws, and nails.

Building the Boat

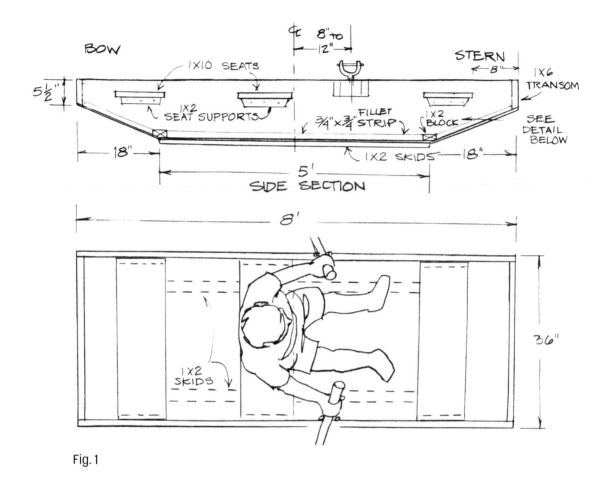

Fig. 1

(See Fig. 1.) Cut the 8' sideboards so they slant down 18" from the ends. Glue and nail the sideboards to the transom ends.

Glue and nail the ¼" plywood bottom to the sideboards.

Glue and nail the ¼" plywood slanted bottom ends to the sideboards and transom ends.

To protect against leaks, cut, glue, and screw two 1×2s where the bottom pieces of plywood join together. This requires shaving ¼" off the bottom edge of the 1×2s to match the angle of the two plywood pieces. **(See Fig. 2.)**

Cut two ¾" x ¾" fillet strips, approximately 9' long, at a 45-degree angle. Glue them in the corners between the side panels and the bottom.

You can make your own oars out of leftover plywood **(See Fig. 3)**, but you will have to buy the oarlocks (www.defender.com).

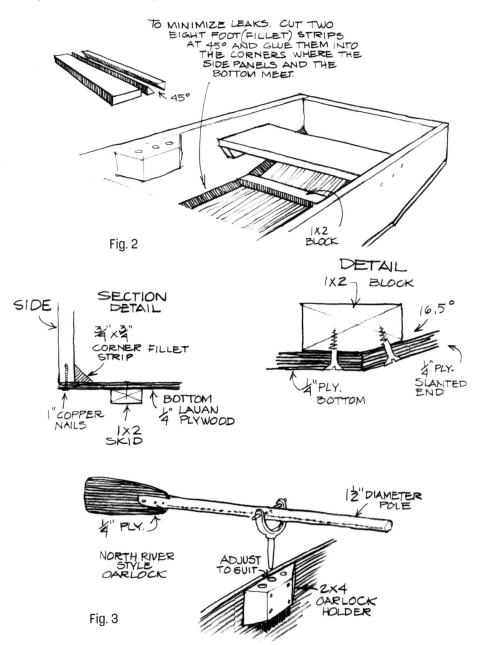

TO MINIMIZE LEAKS, CUT TWO EIGHT FOOT (FILLET) STRIPS AT 45° AND GLUE THEM INTO THE CORNERS WHERE THE SIDE PANELS AND THE BOTTOM MEET.

45°

1X2 BLOCK

Fig. 2

SIDE

SECTION DETAIL

¾" x ¾"
CORNER FILLET STRIP

1" COPPER NAILS

1X2 SKID

BOTTOM
¼" LAUAN PLYWOOD

DETAIL

1X2 BLOCK

16.5°

¼" PLY. BOTTOM

¼" PLY. SLANTED END

1½" DIAMETER POLE

¼" PLY.

NORTH RIVER STYLE OARLOCK

ADJUST TO SUIT

2X4 OARLOCK HOLDER

Fig. 3

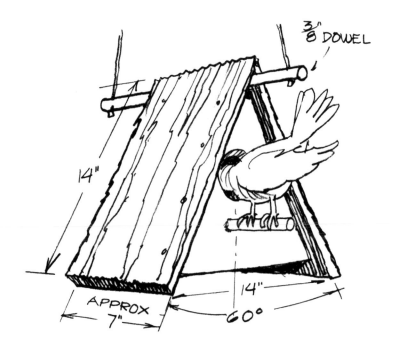

$\frac{3}{8}"$ DOWEL

14"

APPROX
7"

14"

60°

Fig. 1

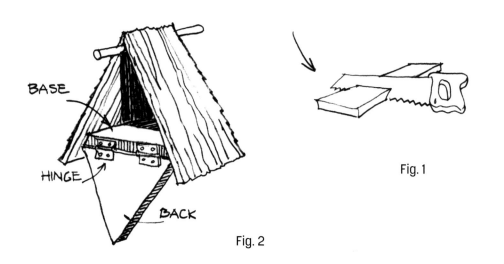

BASE

HINGE

BACK

Fig. 2

BIRDHOUSE

This is a perfect birdhouse to hang near a treehouse, where birds feel right at home. If you are quiet and patient, your perch may allow you to watch the birds up close on their own perch without disturbing them. It is made from two cedar shingles nailed to a wooden base and enclosed by front and back walls.

It is a lot easier to make the base if you have a table or miter saw, set at 30 degrees; however, you can also cut it out using a handsaw, if you are careful. (**See Fig. 1.**)

Hinge the back wall to open out so that you can clean it out each year. (**See Fig. 2.**)

Hang the birdhouse from a branch where squirrels can't get at it. (**See Fig. 3.**)

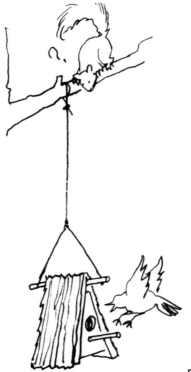

Fig. 3

Ring
Swing
game

RING SWING GAME

This simple game can provide hours of fun. Attach it to a branch near your treehouse. Play it with your friends, family or even by yourself. The object is to let the ring swing and catch itself on the hook. One "hook" out of ten tries is *expert*; one "hook" out of twenty tries is *average*. All you need is a 2" ring, a 4" screw hook, a 1" long screw eye, and a piece of nylon string. Find a branch that is about 8' from the ground. Screw the screw eye to the underside of the branch, 4' from the trunk of the tree. Screw the 4" screw hook to the tree, 5' from the trunk of the tree. Screw the 4" screw hook to the tree, 5' from the ground. Tie one end of the string to the screw hook and the other end to the ring, making sure the center of the ring can pass over the hook when the string is straight. Stand back and hold the ring so that the string is taut and let go. The ring will swing toward the hook on the tree and hopefully catch itself on the hook. *Good luck*!

TARZAN SWING

This is a great way to get wet and cool off fast. All you need is a tree that has a strong branch reaching out over the water and a strong rope. You might even select the spot for your treehouse with this is mind. Tie a loop in the end of a rope and throw it over the branch (using a weight). Place the other end of the rope through the loop and pull it up to the branch. Tie some knots in the bottom end to have something to hold on to.

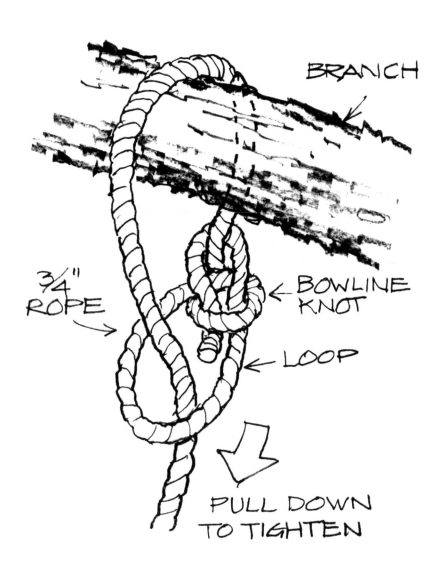

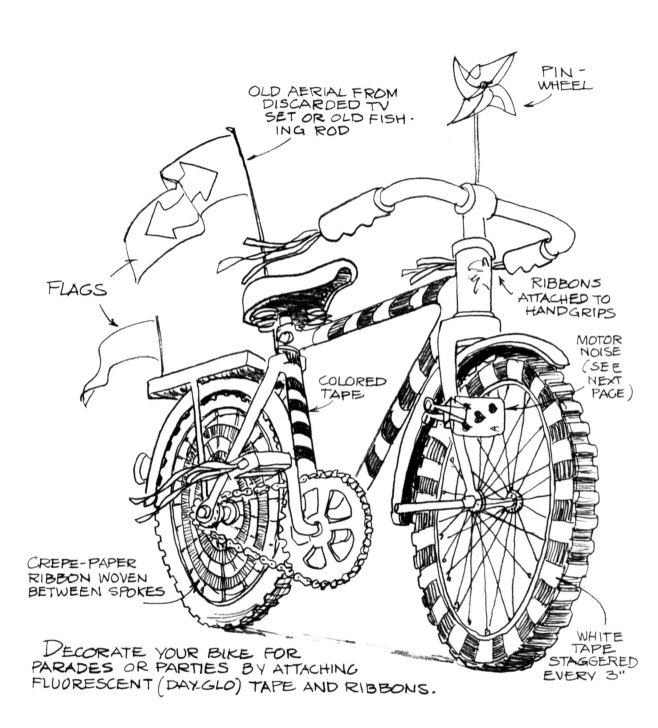

PIN-WHEEL

OLD AERIAL FROM DISCARDED TV SET OR OLD FISH-ING ROD

RIBBONS ATTACHED TO HANDGRIPS

FLAGS

MOTOR NOISE (SEE NEXT PAGE)

COLORED TAPE

CREPE-PAPER RIBBON WOVEN BETWEEN SPOKES

WHITE TAPE STAGGERED EVERY 3"

DECORATE YOUR BIKE FOR PARADES OR PARTIES BY ATTACHING FLUORESCENT (DAY-GLO) TAPE AND RIBBONS.

COOL BIKE DECORATIONS

Make yourself seen and heard in the 'hood with these simple bike decorations.

Motor Noise

Attach a playing card to the bike front fork using a large binder clip. **(See Fig. 1.)**

Bore a hole in the end of the handlebar grip and push the ribbon through with a screwdriver. **(See Fig. 2.)**

Making the Pinwheel (See Fig. 3.)

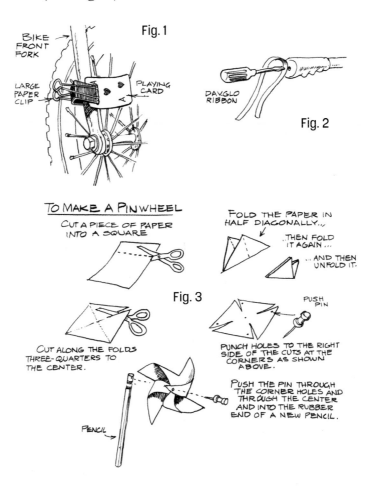

WHEEL OF FORTUNE

This game can easily be made from a discarded bicycle wheel and some old lumber. Attach the wheel to a 2×6 board, using a lag screw and washers. Make the numbers by first cutting out and sticking pieces of 1½"-wide red plastic tape to the tire and then applying white ¾"-wide plastic numbers to the tape. The tape and numbers are sold at most hardware stores. **(See Fig. 1.)**

Cut a rectangular piece from the corner of a plastic milk carton and screw it to the 2×6 board to create a ratchet noise when you spin the wheel and to stop the wheel from turning. **(See Fig. 2.)**

Fig. 1

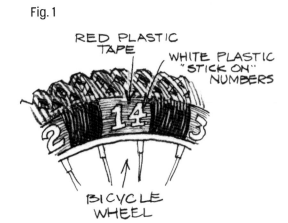

RED PLASTIC TAPE

WHITE PLASTIC "STICK ON" NUMBERS

BICYCLE WHEEL

Fig. 2

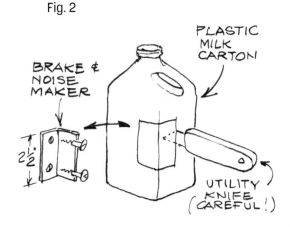

BRAKE & NOISE MAKER

PLASTIC MILK CARTON

UTILITY KNIFE (CAREFUL!)

FOUR SQUARE GAME

Four square is a popular game for kids that can easily be set up on any hard surface. Schools often have this game in their playground, but why not set one up at home? The end of a concrete or asphalt driveway could be used. Another option, if you plan on having this in your backyard, is to cover a plywood base with a thick rubber mat. If you are playing directly on grass, mark off the squares using a chalk block or spray chalk. Although there is no official court size, a typical court measures between 10 and 30' per side, and the court is divided into four equal-size squares. Each square has a rank and is occupied by a single player. Squares can be decorated by the kids with their theme of choice—anything from queens and kings to superheroes. The object of four square is to eliminate other players by bouncing the ball back and forth between quadrants and causing a player in that quadrant to miss the ball. A rubber playground ball is used. Players only use their hands to hit the ball and are not allowed to have prolonged contact with it. The rules are flexible and differ according to kids' ages.

HARD RUBBER
MAT OVER PLYWOOD
BASE

GAGA GAME

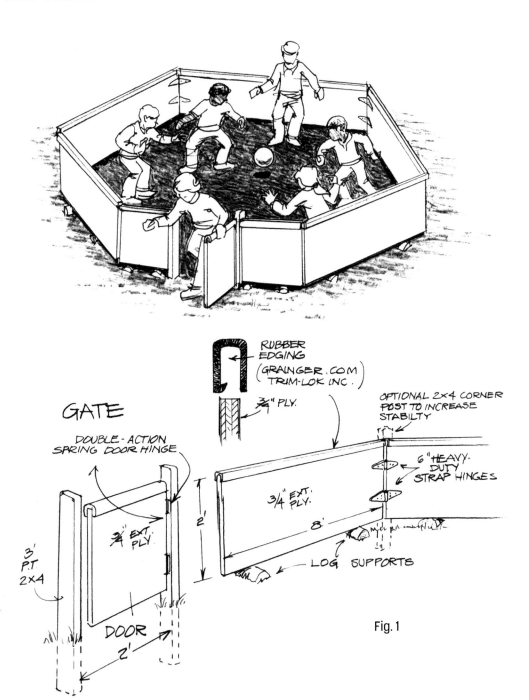

RUBBER EDGING
(GRAINGER.COM
TRIM-LOK INC.)

¾" PLY.

GATE

DOUBLE-ACTION
SPRING DOOR HINGE

OPTIONAL 2×4 CORNER
POST TO INCREASE
STABILTY

6" HEAVY-
DUTY
STRAP HINGES

¾" EXT.
PLY.

¾" EXT.
PLY.

2'

8'

3'
P.T.
2×4

LOG SUPPORTS

DOOR

2'

Fig. 1

Gaga Game

The origins of this popular summer-camp game are uncertain, but it's often said to have originated in Israel ("ga-ga" means "touch-touch" in Hebrew. There's a rival, more specific claim, reported by Stephen Silver in Tablet magazine, that a young camp counselor called Steven Steinberg from Baltimore invented it in 1975. The game is a variant of dodgeball, with the walls of the "pit" originally being benches turned on their sides to stop the ball rolling down a nearby hill. Steinberg says the name came about after he told his six-year-old campers that they looked "like a bunch of babies" and some called back "goo-goo, ga-ga!" There's no denying the game's appeal and popularity, wherever it—or the name—comes from.

The Rules

The rules vary; it's your game and you can make up your own. With that in mind, it goes something like this:

1. At the start, all players in the Gaga pit must be touching the wall. The referee throws the ball into the middle of the pit, where it bounces three times. At each bounce, everyone says "Ga;" after the third bounce everyone says "Ga-Ga-Go!" and the ball is in play.
2. Hit the ball with your open hand, aiming it at another player's leg at or below the knee. If the ball hits or touches anyone at the knee or below, that player is eliminated and must exit the pit. Any contact with the ball at or below the knee also counts.
3. If the ball goes out of the pit, the last person to touch the ball is out.
4. You can only hit the ball once until it touches another player or the wall. You can bounce the ball against the wall, and you can move freely around the pit during play.
5. The game ends when the last person is eliminated.
6. Variations include playing with more than one ball, team games and allowing hits above the knee. You decide!

There are as many variations on pit design as on the rules. Most, but not all, feature solid or slatted walls to let the ball rebound and catch unwary players off guard. Some use rustic logs to define the boundary of the pit and provide unpredictable bounces—if you do this, make sure the gaps between logs are small enough to stop the ball.

It's common to have a simple hinged gate to let the players in and out, or to build one section of the wall lower than the others. Alternatively, screw a cleat or two to a solid wall to give little feet something to scramble up, or leave enough gap between slats for a toehold—we suggest

3–4". In many cases players just step over the walls, which are often only 2–3' high. The lower they are, of course, the more likely it is that the ball will escape.

Typically, the pit is hexagonal or octagonal. The size is up to you. As a guide, eight 8' panels will give you a pit about 19'4" across; 6' panels, a 14'6" pit; 5' panels, 12'; 4' panels, about 9'8".

The playing surface is anything on which a ball can bounce: at its simplest, grass or driveway, compacted sand, or an authentic sea of summer-camp mud. Rubber mats are an option if you want to get serious.

You can easily make a hexagonal Gaga pit by ripping six equal lengths of ¾" exterior plywood, 2' high, and joining them together with ordinary galvanized hinges. On uneven ground, place blocks or logs under the low spots to level the walls. **(See Fig. 1.)** Cover the top of the plywood with rubber edging to protect kids hands when hopping in and out of the pit. (See Grainger.com, Trim-Lok Inc.)

If you're building the pit on grass, you can dig the posts into the ground for stability and permanence. Dig the first post in, as a fixed reference point while you determine the position of the others, but don't backfill the others yet. You don't need concrete, as the walls will support each other, and the holes don't have to be deep—2' is enough.

Acknowledgments

We would like to thank Tony Lyons for his enthusiasm for our book; Abigail Gehring, who supported our vision and was a joy to work with; and Toby Haynes for his incredible editing skills. Thanks also to Toby Haynes and Chris O'Brien, who did a fantastic job building our adventure projects and in some cases also photographing them; and to Simon Jutras whose photographs showed off our Adventure Course to perfection.

Other Books by David and Jeanie Stiles

Backyard Building: Treehouses, Sheds, Arbors, Gates, and Other Garden Projects
Building Small: Sustainable Designs for Tiny Houses & Backyard Buildings
Cabins: A Guide to Building Your Own Retreat
Fun Projects for You and the Kids
Forts for Kids
Rustic Retreats
Sheds: A Do-It-Yourself Guide, 4th Edition
Treehouses You Can Actually Build
Treehouses & Playhouses You Can Build
Treehouses & Other Cool Stuff
Treehouses, Huts & Forts
Workshops You Can Build

Free plans for the cover treehouse are available on our website: www.stilesdesigns.com.
Please visit our site and send us photographs of your projects!

About the Authors

David Stiles is an industrial designer, builder, and illustrator, and Jeanie Stiles is a writer, photographer, and actress. Together they have written twenty-six "how-to" books on backyard building projects that range from treehouses, playgrounds, and garden sheds to tiny houses, workshops, and cabins, and have sold over one million books. They have been called "America's First Couple of Do-It-Yourself Building Projects." They have received several awards, among them the ALA's Notable Children's Book Award for *Treehouses You Can Actually Build*, and their articles have appeared in many magazines and newspapers including *Architectural Digest*, *Better Homes & Gardens*, and the *New York Times*. They have appeared on numerous television programs, including HGTV, the Discovery Channel, and the *Today* show during which they built a treehouse in three hours.

David, a graduate of Pratt Institute and the Academy of Fine Arts in Florence, Italy, received two awards from the New York Planning Commission for his playground design for children with disabilities.